Cambridge Ele

Elements in Psychology and Culture
edited by
Kenneth D. Keith
University of San Diego

TECHNOLOGY AND THE GLOBAL ADOLESCENT

Judith L. Gibbons
Saint Louis University, Missouri
Katelyn E. Poelker
Saint Louis University, Missouri

CAMBRIDGE
UNIVERSITY PRESS

University Printing House, Cambridge CB2 8BS, United Kingdom

One Liberty Plaza, 20th Floor, New York, NY 10006, USA

477 Williamstown Road, Port Melbourne, VIC 3207, Australia

314–321, 3rd Floor, Plot 3, Splendor Forum, Jasola District Centre,
New Delhi – 110025, India

79 Anson Road, #06–04/06, Singapore 079906

Cambridge University Press is part of the University of Cambridge.

It furthers the University's mission by disseminating knowledge in the pursuit of
education, learning, and research at the highest international levels of excellence.

www.cambridge.org
Information on this title: www.cambridge.org/9781108714181
DOI: 10.1017/9781108639538

First published 2020

A catalogue record for this publication is available from the British Library.

ISBN 978-1-108-71418-1 Paperback
ISSN 2515-3986 (online)
ISSN 2515-3943 (print)

Cambridge University Press has no responsibility for the persistence or accuracy of
URLs for external or third-party internet websites referred to in this publication
and does not guarantee that any content on such websites is, or will remain,
accurate or appropriate.

Technology and the Global Adolescent

Elements in Psychology and Culture

DOI: 10.1017/9781108639538
First published online: March 2020

Judith L. Gibbons and Katelyn E. Poelker
Saint Louis University, Missouri

Author for correspondence: Judith L. Gibbons, judith.gibbons@slu.edu

Abstract: Around the world, adolescents use technology for education, to further their identity and socio-emotional development, to access health information, engage in civic activities, and for entertainment. For many, technological advances, especially social media, have drastically influenced how they communicate with family, friends, and romantic partners. Challenges of technology use include the digital divide, internet addiction, and exposure to cyberbullying. The diversity of adolescents' cultural context results in heterogeneous bidirectional influences of technology and teenagers with respect to education and close relationships. Researchers, parents, and policy makers must consider the role of culture in the complex interactions of teenagers with technology.

Keywords: adolescence, technology, social media, identity development, globalization

ISBNs: 9781108714181 (PB), 9781108639538 (OC)
ISSNs: 2515-3986 (online), 2515-3943 (print)

Contents

1 Introduction: The Example of RACHEL

Near the town square and adjacent to a beautiful church, fifteen minutes outside of the colonial city of Antigua, Guatemala, sits a small school. Its structure is simple and, aside from a room with several dated computers, the school does not appear to be well-equipped with twenty-first-century technology or for the tall task of promoting students' digital literacy. However, the school has been outfitted with RACHEL, which stands for Remote Area Community Hotspot for Education and Learning. RACHEL provides students and teachers with access to an abundance of educational resources. This access comes by way of a small wireless router that brings many of the advantages of technology to students who would otherwise be left behind in the digital age (World Possible, n.d.) Students connect to RACHEL just as they would to a wireless network, meaning that they can access content via a cell phone, tablet, or computer. That content includes everything from books to videos of experiments to modules in Khan Academy, an online learning platform designed to provide educational lessons and instructional videos to learners across a variety of disciplines.

RACHEL is the signature initiative of World Possible, an international nonprofit organization dedicated to bringing educational technology to offline learners. In 2008, Norberto Mujica, a systems engineer, visited Ethiopia to teach courses at a university. He was troubled to learn that students had access to computers but not to the vast information available on the Internet. Over the course of several years, Mujica and his team worked to improve access to online resources for students in India, Africa, and Latin America. Although RACHEL is not connected in real time to the Internet, it serves as a hub – an information source for large quantities of educational materials that are refreshed regularly by connecting to an updated server or the Internet. By 2015, RACHEL was being used in thirty-nine countries, and organizations could even buy their own modem online. In 2017, World Possible estimated that they reached 500,000 learners around the world, and the organization continues to add new partner countries and communities.

In preparation for writing this Element, we had the opportunity to talk with the Directors of World Possible in Guatemala, Ghana, and Tanzania, as well as students and a teacher using RACHEL in the Guatemalan school described earlier. RACHEL has a longer history in Guatemala than in most other countries; it was introduced in 2013. Ghana and Tanzania are the two newest members of the RACHEL community; they were added to the World Possible family in 2018. Mustapha and Jackline, the Directors of World Possible in Tanzania and Ghana, respectively, have noticed that some students' grades have

Figure 1.1 Guatemalan students use RACHEL with tablets.

improved already and student attendance has also increased following the introduction of RACHEL into schools there. Jackline mentioned that students benefit from being able to see how each step of a math problem is calculated and from the immediate feedback that the online modules generate, letting students know in real time whether or not they responded correctly. Mustapha emphasized the benefit of RACHEL's virtual library, remarking that students have access to far more books via RACHEL than they ever would have had otherwise. Both Jackline and Mustapha noted how RACHEL has changed the structure of class time. Jackline shared that RACHEL gives teachers the ability to teach using a flipped classroom model in which students do some of the reading and learning *before* coming to class. This means that class time is reserved primarily for active learning in which students apply their knowledge first hand, for example, by conducting experiments. Oscar, the technology director at the school in Guatemala, said that students had completed several projects based on what they had learned from RACHEL, including learning how to recycle food waste by creating compost. In the coming summer months, the Guatemalan students have plans to make artisanal ice cream. In Ghana, the time that teachers previously spent writing notes on the chalkboard is now spent discussing class concepts. This allows teachers more availability to answer students' questions. Two Guatemalan middle school students shared that RACHEL is useful in conducting research for their school projects and papers.

The girls regularly use Wikipedia when they need information about history or theory; it was particularly useful when completing two recent assignments – one on plants and another on evolution. Thus RACHEL allows students to take more ownership and control over their learning.

RACHEL's presence in the schools is also impacting the local communities. In Tanzania, for example, there is a single public library for 600,000 people. According to Jackline, RACHEL has "changed the process of learning and how information is accessed." In both Tanzania and Ghana, young people in the community who have dropped out of school still benefit from RACHEL by accessing community computer labs. In Tanzania, former students attend classes in a church each weekend following Sunday prayers. Students in Guatemala have sold at local gatherings some of the food that they have learned to make via demonstrations on RACHEL, giving the students an opportunity to earn some extra money and showcase their work in the community. In Ghana, students used RACHEL to conduct research on malaria and then presented their research to classmates. After their presentations, they were asked to do small group projects in their communities based on their research. In one favela, students and community members discovered that trenches filled with standing water served as breeding grounds for mosquitos. As a result of this discovery, the community worked to eliminate the water from those trenches, helping to diminish the mosquito population.

RACHEL is unique in that it offers many of the benefits of technology without exposing teens to many of the dangers. The advantages and risks of technology and media access will be discussed in more depth later in this Element, but the resources available through RACHEL provide experience using different technological devices, as well as access to rich educational content, without putting young people at risk of cyberbullying or exposure to predators. So, although RACHEL is only one model to increase adolescents' access to technology, it seems to be a sustainable and resourceful approach. Mustapha summed up RACHEL's impact best – "I am always the happiest guy because of RACHEL. And whenever anyone asks me if I have a girlfriend, I tell them that yes, I do. My girlfriend is RACHEL!"

For many people around the world, technology has taken center stage in their lives. This is particularly true for the world's youth. A recent popular press article revealed the latest trick that US high schoolers are using to instant message in class (Ranosa, 2016). Students use Google's free online word processor, GoogleDocs, to chat back and forth with one another while giving the appearance that they are "working" or "collaborating." By using GoogleDocs' built-in chat and/or comments feature, students can easily and privately communicate with one another and the conversation can then be

Figure 1.2 Students use their cell phones with RACHEL to do homework.

easily deleted if a teacher happens to notice. The creation of such a practice suggests that being "offline," even for an hour or two during class, is untenable.

Adolescents account for 16 percent of the world's population, and youth aged fifteen to twenty-four are the most connected age group when it comes to media (UNICEF, 2017, 2018). Seventy-one percent of young people are online compared to only 48 percent of the total population (UNICEF, 2017). Given that today's adolescents are tomorrow's community and world leaders, parents, and professionals, understanding how media and technology are shaping their daily experiences and relationships, access to educational resources, and goals for the future is essential for developmental scientists, healthcare providers, educators, and parents alike.

Despite the widespread connectivity of today's youth internationally, of course, technology access is not equitable. Although only 4 percent of European adolescents are "offline" (i.e., without regular access to technology), that percentage jumps to 60 percent of youth in Africa. This purpose of this Element is to describe the ways in which technology and media influence adolescents' lives in both the majority world (i.e., developing countries, the global south) and the minority world (i.e., developed countries, the global north). What are the benefits of access and the consequences of a lack of access?

And what about the dangers? Technology does make youth more vulnerable to certain threats and risks. And, moreover, how are young people shaping technology and influencing their families and communities through their technological expertise? In addition, based on the literature, what are the critical next steps regarding adolescents' technology and media usage?

2 Adolescence

Recent estimates from UNICEF suggest that there are 1.2 billion adolescents aged ten to nineteen worldwide (UNICEF, 2018). Adolescence is a developmental period typically defined as the second decade of life. The onset of adolescence is generally equated with the start of puberty and accompanying biological changes. The culmination of this developmental stage corresponds with the assumption of adult roles, which may not occur in minority world countries until the mid-twenties. As Berger (2017) describes it, biology brings about the onset of adolescence, while culture dictates when it culminates. Many developmental scholars argue that the beginning of adolescence is universal, as all young people, regardless of culture or geographic location, experience the hormonal and physical changes associated with puberty. What it means to become an adult in one's society or community, however, varies widely. In other words, adult responsibilities are a loosely defined category and could include everything from finishing school to getting a job to getting married or becoming a parent. Those transitions to adulthood are even more diverse in the majority world, where variable access to economic resources considerably accelerates or delays the transition to adulthood (Juárez & Gayet, 2014).

Evidence from Schlegel and Barry's (1991) analysis of more than 170 societies confirms that adolescence is a (virtually) universal phenomenon. Of the 173 societies with sufficient data for analysis, all had evidence for an adolescent stage for boys and all but one had evidence for an adolescent stage for girls. The exception for girls was the Gros Ventre, an Algonquin-speaking tribe of Native Americans in Montana, USA – a society in which girls marry before menarche and upon marriage assume all of the responsibilities of adult women.

During adolescence, young people around the world experience a host of transitions in the biological, cognitive, and socio-emotional domains of development. As noted above, puberty is a shared cross-cultural experience that makes reproduction possible. It may also be part of the reason that during adolescence "the world expands for boys but contracts for girls," as many parents become concerned for their adolescent daughters' safety and want to keep them from becoming pregnant at a young age (Mensch, Bruce, & Greene, 1998, p. 2). In some cultures, puberty is celebrated with coming-of-age rituals that mark the occasion and signal to the community that the assumption of adult roles is near (Arnett, 2012). Among the most well-known rituals is the *quinceañera* celebration for girls in Latin American cultures – a celebration that marks a girl's fifteenth birthday (Davalos, 1996). Another coming-of-age tradition is the bar and bat mitzvah in Jewish culture (Pargament, Poloma, & Tarakeshwar, 2001).

Cognitively, adolescents make critical advances in abstract thinking and reasoning. Moreover, due to prefrontal cortex development, adolescents are better able to engage in complex social perspective-taking, anticipate consequences of their actions, inhibit inappropriate behaviors and responses, and engage in planning for their futures (Blakemore & Choudhury, 2006). Socially and emotionally, adolescents often use friendships as a bridge between the close parental relationships that characterize childhood and the romantic relationships that define young adulthood. And, although psychologists of the early twentieth century like G. Stanley Hall and Anna Freud promoted the "storm and stress hypothesis" and the inevitable nature of parent-child conflict during adolescence, anthropologist Margaret Mead's (1928) work and more recent research tells us that most adolescents trust their parents, appreciate their advice, and benefit from their support (Arnett, 1999; Hollenstein & Lougheed, 2013; Lerner, 2008). Adolescent-parent conflict is even less common in traditional societies in which families depend on each member for economic contributions (Kağıtçıbaşı, 2017; Offer et al., 1988; Petersen, Silbereisen, & Sorensen, 1996).

Despite the general description of adolescence as a period of transition, many of the specific aspects of this developmental period vary by cultural context. Fortunately, there is a long history of scholarship at the intersection of development and culture. Much of that literature has reported cross-cultural or between-country differences in adolescents' lives (e.g., Gibbons & Stiles, 2004; Kapadia, 2017; Offer et al., 1988). Although those differences certainly exist and are important to acknowledge, it is crucial to remember that there is considerable within-country diversity as well. For example, Guatemala leads the Central American region in economic disparity and is the eleventh most economically disparate country in the world. It is not uncommon to walk into a university classroom in the country's capital city – an experience reserved for the ultra-privileged and elite – and see a room full of new Apple computers and designer shoes and tote bags. On the other hand, a more common scene is a family trying to make ends meet and struggling to pay the enrollment and uniform fees required for their child to attend secondary school. Therefore, it is not difficult to imagine how daily life, including adolescents' challenges and triumphs, varies significantly based on access to economic resources. One of the ways in which daily life differs for adolescents around the world is access to technology and the devices (e.g., computers, smart phones) that make that access possible. In other words, just because adolescents share a nationality or a culture, this does not mean that they should be treated as a homogeneous group – especially when it comes to technology and media access.

3 What are Technology and Media?

Approximately 51 percent of the world's population used the Internet in 2018, totaling 3.9 billion people (International Telecommunications Union [ITU], 2019). The Internet has become almost synonymous with technology, but in the literature, technology and media are commonly referred to by the acronym "ICT" or Information and Communication Technology. But what does ICT mean for adolescents and how is it defined for the purposes of this Element? Generally speaking, ICT encapsulates both the types of media available (e.g., texting, video conferencing, social networking sites) and the devices needed to use that media and technology like computers, smart phones, and tablets. ICT is also described broadly as "any kind of commercial product involved in the electronic transmission of information" (Manago & Pacheco, 2019, p. 2). Electronic gaming is also subsumed under the category of ICT.

Social Networking Sites (SNSs) like Facebook, Instagram, and Twitter comprise a particular subgroup of ICT and are particularly important for adolescents. Although the particulars of each SNS vary, the sites typically share three characteristics (Boyd & Ellison, 2007). First, these online networks allow users to create profiles that can be shared publicly or privately, depending on user preference. Second, SNSs allow users to create virtual networks in which people can connect with others. Those connections may be driven by an actual relationship, shared interests, or some other factor. Third, SNS users can look at their connections' connections (another way to think about "friends of friends") and can grow their own social networks by including those people in their networks as well.

Data from the ITU (2019) reveal overall increasing trends in technology access worldwide. In 2018, there were 107 mobile phone subscriptions for every 100 people; the pattern of having more cell phone subscriptions than people held in both minority and majority world countries. There seems to be more disparity between minority and majority world countries with respect to computers than cell phones. For example, 82 of every 100 minority world households has a computer compared to only 36 of every 100 households in the majority world. Rates are somewhat higher for Internet access at home, with 83 of every 100 minority world households having internet access compared to 48 of every 100 majority world households. Given the pervasiveness of access to technology around the world, parents are even redefining illiteracy. A Syrian mother living in a refugee camp in Jordan remarked, "In my time, someone who was illiterate could not read or write. Now, someone who is illiterate does not know how to use the internet" (UNICEF, 2017, p. 38). Just like the importance of reading and writing in generations past and present, this mother also recognizes the significance of technological literacy for her children's future. "I don't want our children to be illiterate. It's really important. We want a better future for our kids" (UNICEF, 2017, p. 38).

According to 2018 data from the Pew Research Center, 90 percent of adolescents in the United States go online multiple times a day and 45 percent reported being online "almost constantly" (Anderson & Jiang, 2018). In New Zealand, teens' time spent online is comparable, as 33 percent of adolescents reported being online a minimum of four hours a day (Pacheco & Melhuish, 2018). In light of those statistics, it is not surprising that Twenge (2017) has nicknamed members of Generation Z (youth born after 1994) as the "iGeneration" or "iGen." Although Twenge's work is based on US youth, evidence from young people around the world supports her claim. For example, a seventeen-year-old boy from the Democratic Republic of the Congo described himself as part of the "most computerized generation" (UNICEF, 2017, p. 15).

The term "digital natives" is closely related to Twenge's "iGen" label. Coined in 2001 by Prensky, digital natives are people born since 1984 who have grown up with technology ever-present in their lives (Prensky, 2001). According to Prensky's conceptualization, digital natives are technology gurus with an extraordinary aptitude for technology simply because they have been raised in a context in which technology access is ever-present. In other words, he argues that those technology skills are not learned but are inherently known simply because digital natives have never experienced a world without constant technology access. This way of thinking about current and upcoming generations of learners quickly influenced educators around the world, given that Prensky (2001) suggested that educational methods and practices used with earlier generations of students would no longer be effective. However, despite the rapid translation of this idea to the education arena, many critics now refer to the "myth of the digital native" (e.g., Brenoff, 2017; Kirschner & De Bruyckere, 2017). In other words, the empirical evidence does not support this idea of knowing how to navigate technology without learning or practicing those skills (Kirschner & De Bruyckere, 2017). In a study with Italian youth, secondary

Figure 3.1 Twelve-year-old girl from the USA does her homework.

school students accomplished simple technological tasks (consistent with a "cut and paste" approach) well, but they did not meet with success on more complex technical assignments requiring critical thinking about technology (Calvani et al., 2012). Thus the argument against the concept of digital natives is not that today's adolescents do not have technological skill or "know-how" but that their abilities do have limits and are probably not so innately sophisticated as Prensky (2001) had postulated.

In the context of the current Element, we would like to offer a more specific critique of Prensky's concept of the digital native. His idea that unlimited access to technology has been universal for people born since 1984 represents a biased view of the world and probably one rooted in minority world experiences. Although statistics indicate that access to technology and media are increasing internationally, it does not mean that access to or experience with technology is universal for adolescents around the world (Bennett & Maton, 2010; Thinyane, 2010). In sum: (a) simply being raised in a technology-focused culture does not automatically confer knowledge of how to use that technology, and (b) the world's youth still vary widely in their access to and direct experiences with that technology. For example, the students who engage with technology exclusively or primarily through RACHEL during the school day experience technology very differently from young people who have a smart phone, tablet, and/or computer for their own use at home and at school.

Data on adolescents' use of technology are available, but are largely limited to youth living in the minority world. According to the Pew Research Center, YouTube, Instagram, and Snapchat were US adolescents' preferred sites (Anderson & Jiang, 2018). In New Zealand, 40 per cent of adolescents regularly have accounts with at least five different social media sites (Pacheco & Melhuish, 2018). Snapchat emerged as the online platform that US teens reported using most often in 2018 (Anderson & Jiang, 2018). The data also revealed socio-economic status (SES) differences regarding the use of SNS sites; youth from lower-SES families were more likely to use Facebook than their higher-SES peers. US adolescents also differed in their perceptions of the impact of social media on their lives. Most (45 percent) held a neutral view, 31 percent said that social media positively impacted their lives, and 24 percent claimed that the impact had been negative. Of those adolescents who indicated that the media had played a positive role, 40 percent said that it was because it made connecting with family and friends easier. The most commonly cited negative reason (given by 27 percent of respondents who said that social media had a negative effect on their lives) was that social media contributed to cyberbullying and the spread of rumors. In terms of access to devices, approximately 95 percent of US adolescents owned or had access to a smart phone; this number had risen by 22 percent since 2014. Access to a desktop or laptop computer at home was widespread among US adolescents but related to income level; 96 percent of adolescents living in households with an annual income of at least $75,000 could access a computer at home compared to only 75 percent of adolescents living in households with an annual income of $30,000 or less. A similar trend emerged when looking at the relation between computer access at home and parental education levels; parents with higher education levels were more likely to provide home computer access for their adolescent children. The challenges of at-home computer and internet access are probably contributing to the "homework gap" in the USA (McLaughlin, 2016). Children from lower-SES families may struggle to access computer assignments and other resources for their coursework at home because they do not have access to computers and high-speed Internet. This, in turn, puts an already vulnerable group of young people at risk of falling further behind in their academic work.

Adolescents are also influenced by traditional or legacy media (e.g., newspapers, magazines, radio, and television; Twenge, Martin, & Spitzberg, 2018), although scholars debate the extent to which "new media" have replaced teens' interest in traditional media. Using data from the USA-based Monitoring the Future survey with eighth, tenth, and twelfth graders, Twenge et al. (2018) found that US teens are using legacy media less frequently in favor of digital media. Legacy media were defined as going to the movies, watching television, and reading newspapers and magazines. Digital media usage included time spent online engaged in a variety of activities (e.g., emailing, instant messaging, shopping, gaming, searching, and downloading music). Using the displacement model, Twenge et al. (2018) argued that as adolescents spend more time engaged with digital media, they simply have less time to spend interacting with legacy media. Data collected from adolescents in thirty countries across North America and Europe supported the trend of increased adolescent digital media usage from 2002–2010 (Boniel-Nissim et al., 2015). Unfortunately, detailed media usage data from majority world youth are limited, but it is an area that researchers should explore more thoroughly as technology and media become increasingly influential for the world's youth.

4 Technology and Social Change

Adolescents are often on the cusp of social change. In preindustrial societies, adolescents are frequently the source of innovations and change (Schlegel & Barry, 1991). In today's world, young people are using technology to create social change, and, in turn, technology transforms their opportunities, values, and behavior. A recent book and associated film documented the inventiveness of William Kamkwamba of Malawi. At age fourteen, he was forced to leave school because his family could not afford the fees. With scraps of metal and out-of-date science books, he forged together a wind-driven system to bring electricity to his village (Kamkwamba & Mealer, 2009). Another young inventor was sixteen-year-old Kiara Nirghin from South Africa, who developed a polymer made from avocado skins and orange peels. Added to soil, the polymer stores water, allowing plants to better withstand drought. Moreover, as mentioned previously, adolescents with access to information from RACHEL have used it to create new products such as artisanal ice cream and fruit liquor for the economic development of their communities.

Social change has a complex relation to technology: it both drives technological innovation and is propelled by technological advances. The relation between globalization (along with economic development) and social changes such as attitudes, values, and interpersonal behaviors has been the topic of numerous theories and correlational studies. According to classic modernization theory, education and employment in large organizations promote changes in people's thinking and behavior, including greater openness to new experience, increased civic participation, and reduced allegiance to traditional familial and religious hierarchies (Inkeles & Smith, 1974). A current expanded version of the theory, evolutionary modernization theory, provides evidence for consistent value changes that are associated with modernization as well as proposing explanatory mechanisms. The changes in attitudes and values that are associated with modernization and globalization include endorsing greater individual choice and greater equality between women and men (Inglehart, Ponarin, & Inglehart, 2017). The proposed mechanism is that upon achieving economic security, people do not need so large a family. Therefore, survival and success can be achieved without emphasis on fertility. Lower fertility goals allow for gender equality as well as greater acceptance of divorce and homosexuality.

One distinct consequence of modernization and schooling is more rapid cognitive development among children (Gauvain & Munroe, 2009). Children's performance on cognitive tasks in four cultures (the Garifuna of Belize, the Logoli of Kenya, the Newars of Nepal, and the Samoans of American Samoa) was related independently to both schooling and modernization of their community (Gauvain & Munroe, 2009). These findings may be related to the Flynn effect, a robust increase in intelligence over the last century (Flynn, 1987). The Flynn effect has been attributed to the increased complexity in people's lives, which, in turn, may be a consequence of modernization. That is, along with attitudinal changes associated with modernization, intellectual changes may occur as well.

Figure 4.1 Thirteen-year-old adolescent girl and her nine-year-old cousin discover something fun on the Internet.

Another theory of social change proposes a shift from traditional communities (*Gemeinschaft*) to a modern urban lifestyle (*Gesellschaft*; Greenfield, 2016). The changes associated with the transition include more education, greater use of technology, and lower birth rates, as well as endorsement of greater independence and gender equality and less attention to interdependence and respect. Many of those differences have been documented in cross-generational studies. For example, Manago (2014) found that younger generations in evolving Mexican communities were more likely than their parents or grandparents to endorse independence and egalitarian gender roles. In another study framed by Greenfield's theory, younger generations in Arab communities held more individualistic and gender egalitarian attitudes, and girls in urban compared to rural communities also endorsed more individualism and egalitarianism (Weinstock et al., 2015). In both cases, the possession of mobile devices mediated the differences, suggesting that technology is a driver of social change.

The divide between rural and urban settings in Greenfield's theory is echoed in a recent series of interviews with adolescents worldwide. Based on interviews with over 4,000 adolescents from 88 countries, Kimball (2019) argues that the main divide among adolescents is not between genders or between youth of different nationalities but between rural and urban youth. Kimball sees rural youth as left behind in terms of technology and left out of global youth culture.

Other recent approaches to social and personal transitions emphasize that change in various domains is not uniform and that, although shifts may occur in one or more domains, people often hold on to traditional values in areas of importance to them (e.g., Inglehart & Baker, 2000). For example, the major theory of acculturation (Berry, 1980, 1997) proposes that the most adaptive strategy for immigrants is a bicultural one – to develop behaviors, attitudes, and values consistent with the new culture while maintaining the core of one's heritage culture. A more recent theory, cultural fusion theory, also emphasizes the combining of heritage and host cultures and, in addition, proposes the development of interculturality, a fusion forged by both interpersonal and mass communication (Croucher & Kramer, 2017). The strategy of adopting new ideas while maintaining long-standing traditions is apparent in adolescents' responses to technology and exposure to other cultures. For example, Belizean girls, raised with a traditional Caribbean heritage, receive transnational messages through tourism and the media (Anderson-Fye, 2003). In response, they learned to reject normative violence against women and to label gender-based mistreatment as abuse. On the other hand, they rejected media images of pressure to be thin and reported feeling attractive regardless of their weight. This ethnographic study reveals the complexity of a selective response to globalization and Western influences (Anderson-Fye, 2003). As we will outline below, a model that incorporates both value changes and value maintenance best fits the response of adolescents to technology.

5 How Do Adolescents Use Media and Technology?

5.1 Theories of Media Use and Consequences

The major theory of media use is the *uses and gratification* approach (McQuail, 1994). The essence of this theory is that people select and use media in ways that satisfy their social and psychological needs. This theory has been applied to various forms of media – from investigating why people read newspapers (e.g., intellectual stimulation, cultural knowledge, to acquire information and advice for everyday life, reassurance about one's goals and purpose; Katz, Blumler, & Gurevitch, 1974) to why teens like heavy metal music (e.g., for its originality and social consciousness; Arnett, 1991). A correlate of the uses and gratifications theory is that people will react to the same media differently depending on their motivations and personal characteristics. Thus, some of the early studies of the effects of watching violent television programs on adolescents' behavior were carried out among boys in residential care. Those individuals might already be prone to aggressive behavior and might have responded more aggressively to the violent television than would have other groups of youth (Friedrich-Cofer & Huston, 1986).

The uses and gratifications approach to media use has been criticized because individuals may not always have the freedom to choose which media to use. For example, there may be constraints imposed by a lack of technology, censorship from parents or governments, or social pressures to participate in particular media (Ruggiero, 2000). With respect to social pressure on media use, think of the current popularity of the Netflix series *Game of Thrones*. Can individuals who have not watched the series effectively participate in everyday conversations or understand sayings such as "winter is coming"? The theory has also been criticized for a related flaw – being too individualistic. It is based on individual selection of media and decision-making, whereas media decisions can also be made by families, communities, and schools. Despite these criticisms, uses and gratifications is a useful framework for looking at adolescents' use of technology and media across the globe and in a changing world. For example, it is important to understand why some young people choose to use social media such as

Facebook or Instagram and others prefer searching the Internet for information about environmental change or other current issues.

Dani, a fifteen-year-old girl in Guatemala, is an example of the latter; she chooses not to use social media such as Facebook or Instagram. Many of her friends use Instagram, Snapchat, or Tumblr. Although Dani spends about two hours a day on her smartphone or iPad, she uses electronics almost exclusively for schoolwork, including a chatroom where she discusses academic issues and questions with her classmates. Dani may be atypical of today's adolescents, but she thinks that direct experiences with her friends, classmates, family, and people she meets traveling are more important than virtual connections.

Other theories are often used to frame adolescents' interactions with the media, including cultivation theory, media practice theory, and social learning theory. Cultivation theory posits that the use of media forms or contributes to people's worldviews – their assumptions about life and society (Gerbner et al., 1994). For example, fictional stories portrayed on television foster misconceptions of reality in two ways: (1) belief in a just world, that bad people often or always get their due, and (2) belief in a mean world, that the world is a dangerous place. Correlational studies have shown that television viewing is associated with belief in a just world, that people receive the consequences they deserve (Appel, 2008), and that heavy television users view the world as more dangerous and other people as untrustworthy (Roberts & Bachen, 1981). Those constructed worldviews are also sustained through another cognitive function – confirmation bias (Nickerson, 1998). People who believe that the world is a dangerous place will selectively attend to reports that portray that image (e.g., news reports of murders and natural disasters).

Cultivation theory relies primarily on correlational studies, in part, because long-term and pervasive consequences of media use are difficult to study experimentally (Rossmann & Brosius, 2004). Instead, most researchers of cultivation theory rely on a three-step process. First, they conduct a content analysis of the media, second, a comparison of that portrayal with reality, and third, correlations between the use of the medium and beliefs that can either match the media portrayal or the reality. Although this process leads to convincing evidence for relations between media use and beliefs, the question of causality remains unaddressed.

A few studies have experimentally tested the cultivation of beliefs through media viewing. Riddle (2010) exposed university students to television content that varied in the vividness, recency, and frequency of violence. The dependent variables were attitudes about the prevalence of crime, police racism, and police dishonesty. The major finding was that the frequency and vividness of the portrayal of violence interacted to foster a worldview that crime is prevalent and police are likely to be dishonest and racist. This study provided strong support for a cultivation theory of TV violence.

Talk shows are a form of media that in both Germany and the USA often feature sexual and erotic topics. In a cultivation study by Rössler and Brosius (2001), 165 German adolescents (ages fourteen to sixteen) were exposed to either an experimental condition (five talk shows about lesbian or gay male relationships) or a control condition (five talk shows about fashion, beauty, celebrities, and personal future expectations). Teenagers who viewed the shows about lesbian and gay relationships gave higher estimates of the prevalence of gay men and lesbians in the population, perceived public opinion to be more favorable toward those relationships, and held more positive attitudes toward lesbian and gay relationships than did the control group. Those findings are strongly supportive of cultivation theory – that media images affect individuals' perceptions of reality and change their own beliefs. Given that this study occurred in a school environment, those effects might have been partially the result of the educational setting; perhaps the students interpreted the videos as educational content that they needed to learn.

An experimental study about the effects of playing violent video games took place among undergraduate students in Singapore (Chong et al., 2012). Students were randomly assigned to an experimental group or a control group. Participants in the experimental group played a violent video game, *Grand Theft Auto*, twice per week for three weeks for a total of at least twelve hours. Those in the control group did not play any video games during that same three-week period. Following the intervention, the participants who played the violent video game estimated higher numbers of deaths from auto accidents and drug overdoses. However, there was little evidence for change in participants' own attitudes about violence following the exposure.

In a third experimental study of cultivation, over 4,000 US students attending a university near the Mexican border were exposed to fake news reports about immigration or a control condition about the weather (Seate & Mastro, 2016). Those who saw a report about the threats of immigration (e.g., increases in crime and threats to the economy) were less likely to endorse the human rights of immigrants than the control group or those who saw a report about the positive cultural contributions of immigrants to the community. However, attitudes about immigration policy were not affected by the manipulations. This finding implies that viewing a single news report can affect some attitudes toward immigrants but that the effects may not extend to all immigrant-related issues. Overall, the findings support cultivation theory, especially with respect to the media's effect on worldviews about the make-up of society. The evidence for specific changes in individuals' attitudes is more limited.

Media practice theory was developed from observations of US adolescents' bedrooms and their "room culture," the multiple ways in which media were used and expressed in their rooms (Steele & Brown, 1995). The model is based on daily activities of adolescents with respect to media, their lived experiences, and how identity is created and enacted through a dialectical process with the media. Specifically, adolescents' sense of who they are shapes their responses to media, which, in turn, alter or reformulate their identities, which inform their interactions with the media. Those steps are referred to as a circular process of selection, interaction, and application (Steele & Brown, 1995). Throughout the process, adolescents construct and reconstruct their identity through their media interactions. For example, Suzanne said that she liked to read stories about things that had actually happened: "Like if I stop reading ... the story will keep going ... I could really identify with that" (Steele & Brown, 1995, p. 563). Nathan could see himself in a beer ad that showed young adults relaxing on an open porch rather than engaging in extreme partying.

Media practice theory has been applied to the role of media in adolescent development, including sexual development (Brown, 2000) and nutritional health socialization (Te'Eni-Hararia & Eyalb, 2019). With respect to sexual development, adolescents first select media with sexual content because of their emerging sexuality. They adapt the images and messages to their own needs and viewpoints; those viewpoints might differ greatly depending on the teens' own context. For example, black male youth interpreted the lyrics of Madonna's "Papa Don't Preach" as referring to a girl wanting to keep her boyfriend, "baby." White girls thought it was about a teenage girl wanting to keep her unborn baby (Brown & Schulze, 1990). The next step is that adolescents then selectively apply the media messages to their own situation. They may decide, for example, that the sexual behavior depicted represents something they want to adopt or reject. That revised identity as a sexual person then informs their further selection of sexual media.

Adolescents are exposed daily to multiple advertisements for food. In the United States, the average number of food ads viewed by adolescents is over sixteen per day (Te'Eni-Hararia & Eyalb, 2019). Most of those ads are for "junk" food – unhealthy, low-nutrient substances such as candy and soft drinks. Central to most food ads are models that represent thin or athletic bodies, the thin ideal, a physique that is inconsistent with the ingestion of the high-fat, high-sugar products being advertised. Although many adolescents are somewhat critical of advertising, they nevertheless often select media with advertising that is appealing for its portrayal of attractive adolescents and popular celebrities. Their interactions with the media depend on their own motivations; for example, girls may be more vulnerable to adopting the thin ideal than are boys.

In a study of Israeli adolescents' experiences with food ads (Te'Eni-Hararia & Eyalb, 2019), students reported that their eating and exercise habits were influenced by family members, who were most often role models for positive healthy eating habits. Friends were important as exercise or sports companions and for conversations about dieting, but they often shared junk food together. In applying the media messages to their own lived experiences, participants mostly consciously rejected the ad's overt message. For example, a tenth grade boy responded to the 0 percent fat ice cream: "All things that are diet, 0% fat, to really replace the taste of the fat and the sugar and all the tasty things they put all sorts of other products, all sorts of other ingredients that replace the taste and it just comes out disgusting" (Te'Eni-Hararia & Eyalb, 2019, p. 7). Yet despite rejecting the message, they reported succumbing to eating junk food; a seventh grade girl said, "If you're going to eat something unhealthy, at least have it be tasty" (Te'Eni-Hararia & Eyalb, 2019, p. 8). Identity and self-presentation were prominent themes in the teenagers' responses to the food ads. A seventh grade girl commented, "I would not eat even a 30% ice cream in public because it is considered being fat. In my gender, being a girl, I cannot stuff my face with hamburgers next to my friends" (Te'Eni-Hararia & Eyalb, 2019, p. 9). In sum, the application of media practice theory to examine adolescents' responses to food advertisements allows consideration of the complexity of adolescents' interaction with media.

Social learning theory accounts for the effects of media through modeling or through reinforcement of individuals' existing beliefs (Roberts & Bachen, 1981). Social networking sites, for example, may be influential in adolescents' alcohol use (Moreno & Whitehill, 2014). Posts by older adolescents and emerging adults can often be seen by their peers as well as by younger adolescents. The content of alcohol portrayals on Facebook and other social media sites falls most often under the rubric of fun or partying; negative consequences of alcohol use such as hangovers or embarrassment are rarely portrayed (Moreno & Whitehill, 2014). Peer influence or modeling may lead adolescents to imitate their peers' depictions of alcohol use and their offline actual use of alcohol. Social learning theory has also been used to describe adolescents' response to media portrayals of sexuality (Brown, 2002). For adolescents in the USA, the media is the third or fourth most common source of information about sex (after friends, parents, and sometimes school). Sexuality as portrayed in the media differs from reality in the attractiveness of the actors, the absence of use of protection, and the often-fleeting relationships between the sex partners. Social learning theory predicts that people will imitate behavior in which the models are rewarded for the behavior (often the case in media portrayals of sexuality;

Brown, 2002). The media may also provide behavioral scripts for sexual behavior; scripts that might be adopted, especially by inexperienced youth. Thus modeling may account for at least some of media's effects on adolescents.

A vivid example of direct imitation of film characters by teens occurred in 1993 (Arnett, 2010). In the Disney film *The Program*, several teenage football players demonstrated their toughness by lying down in the middle of a busy highway as cars and trucks sped by. In three reported incidents, adolescent boys were seriously injured or killed when they copied the stunt. Direct copying of dangerous behavior is, fortunately, rare. Arnett concluded from his analysis that fewer than 1 in 400 people who saw the film imitated the highway scene. Why some teens are drawn to copy the behavior they see but most are not deserves further attention.

5.2 How Adolescents Use Media

Under the framework of the uses and gratifications model, Arnett has outlined five uses of media by adolescents (Arnett, 1995). Those include: entertainment, identity formation, high sensation seeking, coping, and youth culture identification. The entertainment function of media is clear; for example, teenagers can often be seen with headsets, listening to their favorite music. However, an often-overlooked function of media for adolescents is identity formation. Teenagers' identification with a particular type of music, such as punk, hip-hop, or rap, can constitute a central part of the self-concept (Frith, 1996). In a study of adolescents in Hong Kong, positive identity development in the domains of personal growth, health, community, and social identity was associated with media use (Cheung, 2016). Social media, in particular, allow for exploration of identity through constructing various self-presentations (Uhls, Ellison, & Subrahmanyam, 2017). Adolescents are high in sensation-seeking, and the popularity of action films among adolescent boys may reflect a sensation-seeking motive (Arnett, 1995). Teenagers may also use media as a coping strategy; Larson (1995) pointed out that for US adolescents, solitary media use may provide a way to deal with stress, sadness, and anger. The final use of media by adolescents may be that which is expanding most rapidly – for identification with youth culture around the world.

Although Arnett's list of five uses of the media by adolescents is valuable, it is not exhaustive. An obvious use of the media, especially the Internet, by adolescents is simply for acquiring information. In fact, RACHEL, the apparatus introduced by World Possible, is used almost exclusively for this purpose. Although RACHEL could be used to access books and videos for entertainment, students primarily use RACHEL to research topics for their projects.

Figure 5.1 Thirteen-year-old US boy checks his cell phone for messages.

Dani, the Guatemalan adolescent mentioned earlier, although she has daily access to the Internet, uses it only for gathering information for schoolwork and communicating with classmates about assignments.

5.3 Global Youth Culture

A global youth culture is emerging, fueled by the Internet. Most conspicuous among connected global youth are the elements of expressive culture, "the aesthetic, ritual, and leisure time pursuits of a category of people" (Schlegel, 2000, p. 71). For adolescents, those include music preferences, modes of dressing, and self-presentation on social media, as well as speech patterns and use of slang. An example of a ritual holiday that has spread from the West to teenagers in Poland is the celebration of St. Valentine's Day (Schlegel, 2000). Not part of traditional Polish culture, the holiday has swept through college-preparatory schools, with events organized by students. Moreover, like most cultural rituals, it has been transformed to meet local preferences or needs; among Polish youth, the focus is entirely on romantic relationships (excluding platonic friendships), with Valentine's Day messages sent mostly by adolescent girls to boys.

However, although expressive culture is the obvious part of the global youth culture, it may not reflect the core. Kimball's interviews with over 4,000 teens in 88 countries revealed a strong affiliation among youth from around the world.

However, her participants emphasized not only commonalities in clothing and music tastes but also a shared commitment to social movements and environmental protection (Kimball, 2019). Their most important goals were not materialistic but instead the desire to do good. They were especially concerned with addressing climate change and economic inequity. These findings correspond to those of Gibbons and Stiles (2004), who, in surveys of over 8,000 adolescents from 21 countries, found that adolescents most valued kindness, honesty, and prosocial behavior in the ideal person; having a lot of money or being sexy were rated as much less important.

What all three perspectives on the global youth culture (i.e., Arnett, 1995; Schlegel, 2000; Kimball, 2019) have in common is that access to the media, especially the Internet, allows adolescents a great deal of freedom and choice. Arnett argues that the choice of type of media, its content, and young people's motivation for engaging with the media create an opportunity for adolescents to engage in self-socialization. Instead of being subject to outside influences, such as families, schools, and communities, teens actively socialize themselves through their media use. Schlegel (2000) emphasizes the agency of many adolescents in becoming part of the global adolescent culture but points out that, consistent with the uses and gratifications model, adolescents bend it to their own purposes. Kimball (2019) points out that adolescent freedom in the use of the Internet and cell phones allows youth to share information rapidly and that this has empowered young people's political movements in places as diverse as Tunis, New Delhi, Hong Kong, and Paris.

6 Adolescent Identity and Globalization

The global youth culture has transformed the process of adolescents' identity development; today's youth must approach identity development differently than their peers did in the past (Jensen & Arnett, 2012). Young people with access to the global youth culture must negotiate potential tensions between those values and lifestyles and those promoted by their traditional cultures. Jensen and Arnett (2012) apply the acculturation model of Berry (1980, 1997) to the process that teens undergo when faced with globalization and exposure to new ways of being. They can choose to assimilate, shedding their traditional ideas and cultures and adopting the global youth culture. Some adolescents take a different approach, rejecting outside influences and adhering strictly to the traditional beliefs and practices of their local culture. The third strategy is marginalization, rejecting both the values of global youth culture and traditional culture. However, the most common, and possibly the most adaptive, strategy is integration, an often-creative means of combining the traditional with the modern, the local with the global.

Kağıtçıbaşı (2005) offers a complementary model to Jensen and Arnett's (2012) hybrid identity and Berry's (1980, 1997) bicultural identity – an autonomous-related representation of the self. Socialization for an autonomous-related conceptualization of the self begins in childhood and reflects shifting cultural values that support both an individual identity and a commitment and connectedness to one's family. In short, her approach provides another model for the melding of two value systems, often spurred by a changing society. Taken together, the models of a hybrid identity, bicultural identity, and autonomous-related self suggest that many young people are navigating a world in which they must reconcile (at least) two often-divergent value systems.

Among the many examples of adolescents' use of the integration strategy are Armenian adolescents, who are living in a country undergoing rapid social change (Huntsinger, Shaboyan, & Karapetyan, 2019). In the six years from 2008 to 2014, the number of Armenians with access to the Internet grew from 6 percent to 46 percent (Huntsinger et al., 2019). In a recent study, there were differences in attitudes about gender roles in marriage between urban and rural adolescents and between those who used the Internet and those who did not; urban adolescents and Internet users held more egalitarian perspectives. Although teens continued to hold beliefs associated with their local identities (interdependence, the importance of extended family, and maintaining family traditions), those ideas were more prevalent among rural adolescents and those who reported less internet use. Urban adolescents held less interdependent self-construals, and almost one-fourth of them said that they did not plan to marry, a distinct departure from traditional Armenian culture. The authors concluded that, "At this point in time, Armenian adolescents are engaging with the global culture, but also retaining the essence of their local culture (Huntsinger et al., 2019, p. 14).

Ferguson, Ferguson, and Ferguson (2017) have referred to the process of incorporating values and identities from another culture as "remote acculturation." Largely through the media, and without international travel, adolescents can be exposed to other ideas and foreign cultures. For example, Jamaican adolescents are exposed to US diets high in fat, salt, and sugar through cable TV advertising as well as from US-style fast food restaurants. Adolescents in Jamaica who watched a higher than average amount of US-based TV were more likely to express a bicultural American-Jamaican identity and also to eat unhealthy foods rather than the traditional Jamaican diet (Ferguson et al., 2018). In another study of remote acculturation, Mexican youth, acculturated to US values by media exposure, held more positive views toward cigarette smoking than did their peers who maintained their Mexican cultural values (Lorenzo-Blanco et al., 2019). Ironically, despite US media depictions of smoking, US adolescents smoke less than their Mexican counterparts (World Health Organization, 2014).

The construction of hybrid identities (the bicultural approach) is one way of coping with the potential friction between the values of global youth culture and those of local communities (Jensen & Arnett, 2012). The particular strategy might involve either code switching (adopting different identities in different situations) or integrating one's identities into a coherent whole, labeled a simultaneous or dual identity by White (2017). An inventive name for this approach was coined by Indian adolescents who termed this process creating a "remixed" identity (Rao et al., 2013). Another metaphor that has been applied to the blending of cultural elements is that of the "palimpsest" (Barbero, 2002). A palimpsest is an ancient manuscript that has been reused but still bears traces of the earlier writing. Thus adolescents remake their identities upon exposure to the globalized world, but the earlier version is still discernible. For example, today's Guatemalan adolescents have adopted some of the values of their peers from the minority world, such as the importance of sexiness in the ideal person; however, they retain other core values such as the high importance placed on family (Flores, Gibbons, & Poelker, 2016).

7 Benefits of Adolescent Technology and Media Use

The benefits that adolescents receive from technology and media access are many. In other words, the advantages of adolescent media use are numerous and diverse, reflecting the myriad ways that young people use and interact with media in their daily lives. As discussed in this Element and emphasized by the Syrian refugee mother and the RACHEL project participants quoted earlier, access to media and technology is helping some of the world's youth to compete on a global platform. In other words, simply having the opportunity to engage with online resources and technological devices opens doors for young people with respect to their futures. But beyond the general benefits of promoting overall digital literacy, there are more specific advantages for adolescents such as the use of social media as an avenue to build social competence, the sharing of health information, and the delivery of health intervention programs.

7.1 Health Interventions

Using technology to deliver health intervention content has been a common way to promote positive media usage among the world's adolescents and address challenges related to their physical and mental health. In Ghana, researchers assessed the impact of two types of text messaging programs on adolescent girls' reproductive health (Rokicki et al., 2017). One was unidirectional (i.e., adolescents only received messages) and the other was interactive (i.e., adolescents both sent and received messages). Findings revealed that, compared to the control group, participants in both intervention conditions reported increased knowledge of reproductive health issues. Both intervention conditions also led to fewer self-reported pregnancies for sexually active girls.

A review summarizing the effects of technology-based interventions on sexually transmitted infections (STIs) and unintended pregnancies incorporated results based on more than 11,000 participants from the USA, China, Australia, the Netherlands, and Uganda (Widman et al., 2018); findings were consistent with the results reported in Ghana. The diverse technology-based interventions reported by Widman et al. (2018) not only promoted greater sexual health knowledge and safe sex attitudes but also increased behaviors associated with safe sex practices, like using a condom. The beneficial effects were stronger during a short-term follow-up compared to a longer-term one (i.e., six months or more), implying that benefits may be relatively short-lived. The results did not differ by country, age, or gender of participants.

The Internet can also serve as a resource for health information but, of course, is only useful when the information provided is accurate. From a public health perspective, young people around the world are those who most need to understand how STIs are contracted and how they can recognize symptoms (Satterwhite et al., 2013). In a qualitative study with US high school and college students, participants shared that discussing sexual health with close others – their parents and peers – as well as with health care providers is uncomfortable, citing a stigma that surrounds these types of conversations (Jones et al., 2018). A Facebook site was recommended by participants as an alternative source of knowledge. For example, one participant shared, "I like the anonymity of the internet" (Jones et al., 2018, p. 13). Another suggestion was to create a separate website to educate young people on sexual health. Participants were particularly interested in having information such as "risk factors, transmission, prevention, signs/symptoms, testing, and treatment" accurately but briefly presented (Jones et al., 2018, p. 14). They also recommended using games as well as testimonials from peers diagnosed with STIs as engaging ways to convey information online. Regarding age differences, participants felt that adolescents would be more amenable to such a website than their emerging adult peers, suggesting that such resources should be constructed with a developmental perspective.

Other interventions have focused on additional domains of adolescent mental and physical health. Researchers have done an excellent job of utilizing and evaluating technology-based interventions to address some of the most pressing health challenges facing today's youth. For example, text messaging was successfully used with older adolescents and emerging adults in New Zealand to reduce depressive symptoms and increase subjective well-being (Arps, Friesen, & Overall, 2018). For twenty-eight days, participants in the gratitude condition received a text message prompting them to think about the gratitude that they felt in a specific aspect of their lives (e.g., their relationships). Youth in the control condition were prompted daily via text message to reflect on things like their hobbies and interests. Despite the intervention's effectiveness, the researchers noted some challenges in implementing such programs, specifically that the high volume of messages (more than 11,000) was resource intensive.

Mental health following natural disasters has also been a target of technological interventions. Researchers used an internet-based program, Bounce Back Now (BBN), to foster adolescent and parental mental health following tornadoes in the US states of Alabama and Missouri (Ruggiero et al., 2015). Participants were randomly assigned to one of three conditions: (1) BBN with content for both adolescents and parents focused on adolescent mental health, (2) BBN with the same content as in the first condition and seven additional modules that specifically addressed parental mental health, and (3) an online assessment-only control condition. Results indicated that adolescents in the two experimental conditions reported fewer PTSD and depressive symptoms at a twelve-month follow-up compared to the control condition. The experimental and control groups did not differ on alcohol consumption at the twelve-month follow-up. Finally, in contradiction to the original hypothesis, adolescents in the BBN-only condition fared better than their counterparts in the BBN plus parental mental health condition, perhaps because in the former group parents focused more exclusively on bettering the lives of their adolescent children as opposed to dividing their efforts between their children and themselves.

7.2 Promoting Physical Activity

Promoting physical activity among young people has been the focus of another set of interventions. A review of nine studies with children and adolescents from minority world countries (e.g., Australia, the United Kingdom, and the United States) concluded that technology-based interventions were effective in promoting physical activity among young people (Lau et al., 2011). The technology used to deliver the intervention included the Internet, email, and text messaging. Interventions were most effective when they also included a face-to-face component. Although a variety of psychological techniques and strategies were used to promote change via technology, behavior change technique (BCT) was the most common. BCT incorporates goal setting and self-monitoring of one's behavior. In seven of the nine studies, participants reported positive psychological and/or behavioral changes (e.g., daily levels of physical activity). The evidence was more consistent for psychological benefits compared to behavioral ones. However, the absence of a control group in most studies limits the ability to make causal inferences.

7.3 Emotion Regulation and Coping

Emotion regulation as an adolescent coping strategy (Arnett, 1995) may also be enacted through social media (Vermeulen, Vandebosch, & Heirman, 2018). Social media has been called "a new platform for emotion regulation" (Vermeulen et al., 2018, p. 212). Interviews with Belgian adolescents revealed that different social media sites were used to express different types of emotions. For example, Facebook, Instagram, and Snapchat were used primarily for sharing positive, joyful feelings. Adolescents reported that receiving "likes" on their posts helped to intensify positive feelings, suggesting that public validation and recognition from others (probably their peers) promotes positive emotional well-being. In a separate study with Dutch youth, negative feedback on social media posts and activity was associated with lower levels of well-being and self-esteem (Valkenburg, Peter, & Schouten, 2006). Twitter use was more often associated with negative emotion expression. A sixteen-year-old girl shared this example: "when I'm happy I will be less inclined to post something on Twitter than when I'm angry or sad or whatever, hurt or something. Most often . . . when I'm sad I most often tweet something about it" (Vermeulen et al., 2018, p. 216). By sharing negative emotions, adolescents are engaging in a type of emotion regulation and coping. The benefits of emotion disclosure (e.g., writing about your negative feelings) have long been supported in the literature (e.g., Pennebaker, 1997).

Adolescents shared that Facebook's private messaging application, known simply as "Messenger," along with text messaging, allowed for the communication of mixed emotions, probably because content is communicated privately between the sending and receiving parties (Vermeulen et al., 2018). In other words, the privacy is likely to promote more honest sharing of adolescents' feelings. The "invisibility" that these modes of communication afford carries both advantages and disadvantages. More specifically, the inability to perceive others' nonverbal responses can both help and hinder communication. A sixteen-year-old boy shared:

> Sometimes I find it easy to share negative emotions face-to-face as well, but sometimes also via chat and the like. Mostly because I am crying and then they will not see that. I do not want, well ... because I do not want that they see ... that it would look vulnerable or anything. (Vermeulen et al., 2018, p. 218)

A fourteen-year-old girl worried that a lack of insight into others' nonverbal responses could lead to miscommunication:

> With chat, you cannot see each other and something can look completely different than you meant it. In real life, you can see each other's face and the way you say it. With chat, yeah, it can look completely different or people could understand it differently. (Vermeulen et al, 2018, p. 218)

Thus the emotions shared via social media appear to depend on which platform the adolescent is using. Sharing positive experiences and feelings openly seems to be a common and beneficial practice. However, negative or mixed emotions are more commonly shared in more private contexts. This pattern has broader implications beyond the sharing of personal emotions. In other words, by sharing positive emotions publicly and reserving the negative for more private venues, adolescents falsely amplify the positivity in their lives. This artificial inflation of positive events makes social comparison likely, as other adolescents probably overestimate the ratio of positive to negative events in their friends' lives. In a 2015 study assessing the relation between Facebook use and depression among US college students, envy emerged as a mediator (Tandoc, Ferruci, & Duffy, 2015). More specifically, Facebook usage and depression were only positively associated when spending time on Facebook incited feelings of envy or coveting another person's possessions, talents, or experiences.

7.4 Empathy and Social Development

In addition to social media's role in regulating and sharing emotions, researchers have also addressed how adolescents' engagement with social media may be related to empathy – the capacity to not only understand what others are feeling but to also experience those sentiments (Vossen & Valkenburg, 2016). In a longitudinal study with Dutch early adolescents, researchers surveyed ten- to fourteen-year-olds about their social media usage (e.g., Facebook, Twitter, WhatsApp) and cognitive and affective empathy levels at two time points one year apart. Cognitive empathy is oftentimes defined as perspective-taking ("I can tell when someone acts happy, when they actually are not"), whereas affective empathy is rooted in feelings ("When a friend is scared, I feel afraid"; Vossen & Valkenburg, 2016, p. 120). Greater social media use at the earlier point in time predicted greater affective and cognitive empathy a year later. More specific investigations of how empathic skills honed on

Figure 7.1 Thirteen-year-old from the USA intently studying her tablet.

social media can be applied to in-person (i.e., nonvirtual) relationships should be prioritized in future research. In light of the findings of Vermeulen et al.'s (2018) study on social media and emotion regulation with Belgian youth and the results of the results of the Vossen and Valkenberg (2016) study with Dutch adolescents, it seems social media platforms are an effective avenue for youth to develop social skills that could enhance interpersonal relationships.

Findings from another study with adolescents suggest that technology, via a video game, can be used as a tool to promote socio-emotional development – specifically, the development of emotional intelligence (Cejudo, López-Delgado, & Losada, 2018). Spanish adolescents were trained in a video game named *Spock* and played the game once a week for ten weeks. In the game, players had to navigate a series of hypothetical intra- and interpersonal situations after learning about the particular context or details of the situation. They then selected the appropriate response to the situation from the options presented to them. Compared to a control group, both boys and girls in the experimental condition reported higher emotional intelligence scores at follow-up. Thus, although video games are often labeled as negative or problematic for young people, especially when violence is a common theme (e.g., Gentile & Gentile, 2008), this study suggests that playing prosocial video games may be an effective intervention tool for promoting adolescents' social and emotional development.

Evidence from Spanish adolescents on the Spanish SNS Tuenti suggested that engaging on that site was associated with higher self-esteem and subjective well-being (Apaolaza et al., 2013). Tuenti was once the most popular SNS in Spain; membership was available by invitation only to people aged fourteen years and older, although many users were younger than age fourteen. Tuenti was the preferred SNS for staying in touch with close friends, while Facebook was utilized for connecting with acquaintances (Monge Benito & Olabarri Fernández, 2011). In other words, Tuenti was not used by Spanish teens as a way to broaden their social networks but was instead used to strengthen existing real-life relationships. It seems that the strengthening of these inter-personal relationships through virtual means helped bolster adolescents' sub-jective well-being via enhanced self-worth and reduced loneliness. One important clarification is that the need for excessive positive self-presentation or an underlying sense of competition is not so central with Tuenti use because teens are simply trying to stay connected with close others as opposed to growing a larger but less intimate social network on Facebook. Thus, in reference to the uses and gratification approach (McQuail, 1994), there may be different associations between SNS usage and well-being as a result of how and why a social media platform is being used.

Like increases in empathy, bolstering social competence may be another way that social media promotes adolescents' social and emotional development by strengthening relationships with others and also by contributing to identity development (Valkenburg & Peter, 2008). Dutch adolescents who used social media as a platform to engage with many online communication partners also had higher levels of social competence, while peers not engaging with such diverse others via online communication did not report the same levels of heightened social competence. In other words, SNSs may be an avenue for adolescents to broaden their horizons in terms of their social relationships as well as have diverse conversations and encounters that shape their own identities. In a related study, also with Dutch teens, instant message use over time fostered adolescents' ability to form new offline friendships (Koutamanis et al., 2013). This benefit was especially true for young people who engaged with many different contacts via instant messaging over time. That finding is not surprising given Valkenburg and Peter's (2008) conclusion described above that teens who communicate with more people via social media also have higher levels of social competence.

7.5 Identity Development

Recall that identity development is one central way in which adolescents use media to advance their development (Arnett, 1995). Identity development via internet usage is undertaken for a variety of reasons, including self-exploration to "test out" how others respond in certain situations, social compensation as a means to conquer shyness, and as a form of social facilitation to encourage relationship formation (Valkenburg, Schouten, & Peter, 2005). In light of the ways in which internet use can serve adolescent identity development, it is not surprising that the youth who may be at risk of loneliness are especially likely to utilize the Internet as a tool when constructing their identities during adolescence (Leung, 2011). Online identity exploration may allow those youth more flexibility than they would enjoy in real-life settings. For example, the Internet may be a space for them to experiment with multiple identities or to escape from their daily challenges. In a study with Chinese youth, identity experimentation via the Internet mediated the relation between social support and a preference for online social interaction (Leung, 2011). More specifically, those participants with lower levels of offline social support were more likely to engage in identity exploration online. Those who were more likely to engage in identity development online reported a greater preference for online interaction. In a study with Australian youth aged eighteen to twenty-five, young men who reported greater social anxiety and less sophisticated identity statuses were more likely to spend time on the Internet (Mazalin & Moore, 2004). In particular, that internet use amounted to more time spent on chatrooms, gaming, and browsing to explore personal interests. Similarly, Israeli adolescents who reported a less clear understanding of their self-concept reported more internet use, suggesting that those adolescents may be using the Internet as a resource in their quest for identity achievement (Israelashvili, Kim, & Bukobza, 2012).

A now-classic study with US adolescents revealed the important role that teens' bedrooms play in helping them to develop and exercise their media preferences (Steele & Brown, 1995). During their tours of adolescents' bedrooms given by the teen participants themselves, Steele and Brown (1995) detected that teenagers were using their bedrooms as a showcase of their media preferences that, in turn, reflected their emerging identities. One sixteen-year-old shared, "I think you can express yourself through, like fragrances and music" (Steele & Brown, 1995, p. 568). Bedrooms not only afforded adolescents a space to showcase their media "style" but to also engage with their preferred media (e.g., by listening to music). These data also support the notion that many adolescents and the process of their identity development are influenced daily in numerous ways by the media around them – from the song that wakes them up each morning via the alarm on their cell phones to the music they stream while heading to school, to the latest Netflix show or Instagram account teens discuss over lunch in the cafeteria.

The role of media in identity development may be especially prominent for youth who identify as a member of a sexual minority group (LGBTQ – lesbian, gay, bisexual, transgender, queer; Craig & McInroy, 2014). A sample of LGBTQ Canadian youth shared that the support from the online community along with the resources that they provided were especially meaningful during their coming out process. A twenty-one-year-old gay cisgender man remarked:

> YouTube actually played a really big role in [my] coming out. I always tell people the six months to a year before I came out was literally a YouTube quest to find coming out videos basically, people telling their stories and the challenges they faced or how happy they are now that they've done it. (Craig & McInroy, 2014, p. 101)

Several participants explicitly shared that they were appreciative of the ways in which the Internet allowed them to pursue identity exploration anonymously. An eighteen-year-old transgender boy shared:

> [Because] online, you can take on any identity you want. You can pick any username, you can pick any gender, any sex, any age, any fake email you want and that opens up a host of opportunities to explore your identity more ... And, when you were alone in the room away from your parents, away from the pressures of school, away from your friends, when you haven't come out to anyone, when your brain is given that choice ... You can create a whole new identity. (Craig & McInroy, 2014, p. 102).

Adolescent immigrants may also be another subgroup of youth that are poised to benefit from using the Internet to foster identity development. In a study with teens from the former Soviet Union now living in Israel, adolescents used the Internet in a variety of ways to help them navigate their transition to their new country (Elias & Lemish, 2009). For example, participants shared that websites created by other immigrants from the former Soviet Union help provide much-needed information about living in Israel. Listening to the news on television or on the radio in Russian helped adolescents to feel empowered about their new country. A twelve-year-old girl who had been living in Israel for 1.5 years said:

> First of all, when I came here, I entered Google and read the news about Israel. Through the news I discovered that in Israel there are sports, concerts. I discovered that Israel is not a completely different world. It gave me a sense of security that I am not in a totally foreign world. I thought that I will need to learn everything anew, but it turned out that the difference is only in the language. (Elias & Lemish, 2009, p. 6)

The Internet not only provided adolescents with more factual knowledge about their adopted country but also helped to serve as resource for pop culture.

The numerous references to pop culture throughout this Element support its relevance for adolescent identity development. A sixteen-year-old participant remarked specifically on the important role of music when navigating the cultural transition and creating an identity in an Israeli context with Russian heritage:

> When I arrived in the country, I found Israeli music on my own on the internet. When surfing at Zvuki.ru [a Russian musical website], I found that they had a category called "Israeli Music." I entered, listened, and loved it. I was particularly interested in what they wrote there about Israeli music and since then I download Israeli songs from this site. (Elias & Lemish, 2009, p. 7)

In addition to providing information about their new home, the Internet also provided a portal to Russian culture, which helped the youth to balance a connection with their homeland and their new life in Israel. Several adolescents reported feeling a sense of pride and superiority about their Russian culture. The Internet helped them to stay connected to that sense of their identity. The ways that the adolescents maintained connections were diverse and including using the Internet to find photos of Russian pop culture icons and Russian landscapes to serve as computer wallpaper.

Lastly, as was the case with LGBTQ youth, the Internet provided a safe space to experiment with new identities. Adolescents found the Internet especially useful for learning more about Jewish aspects of their identity in an Israeli context. Another important aspect of identity development, especially for teen girls, was related to the new standards for beauty in Israel. Several girls suggested that they used the Internet to better understand beauty in Israeli culture and to research ways to assimilate to those standards, which often caused some distress. In sum, the ability to engage in role play with various aspects of their identity while navigating a novel cultural environment provided adolescent immigrants with an important platform for creating a sense of self.

7.6 Civic Engagement, Advocacy, and Activism

Adolescents around the world have been successfully using social media and technology to become more civically engaged. In response to the corruption that has characterized the government in Brazil, thousands of Brazilian youth used SNSs to organize countrywide protests to speak out against corruption (UNICEF, 2017). In one city, Brasilia, seventeen-year-old Jimmy Lima successfully used social media to assemble more than 15,000 anticorruption protestors. In 2009, Pakastani teen Malala Yousafzai began her advocacy work by blogging for the BBC using a pseudonym (UNICEF, 2017). In her blog, Malala highlighted the injustice of girls being denied an education by the Taliban. When her identity was revealed in 2012, she was seriously injured. Malala's determination and continuing advocacy for oppressed girls and women throughout her recovery inspired many around the world. In 2014, she was awarded a Nobel Peace Prize for her efforts. Thus, it seems that social media can be used to harness a generation of youth who are ready to become engaged and act to address some of the world's injustices.

The above anecdotes are certainly compelling, but it is important to understand in more detail how exactly technology, and social media platforms in particular, can be used to promote civic engagement, advocacy, and activism among the world's youth. According to Thackeray and Hunter's (2010) framework, technology contributes to advocacy among youth in five central ways. The first is to help recruit people to participate in the case. The second is closely related to the first – organizing those newfound devotees. Third, beyond the pragmatic is the need to help raise awareness surrounding the cause and also help to influence others' beliefs so that they, too, approach the issues with a similar viewpoint. Fourth, social media can also be used to help raise funds to support an initiative, cause, or project. The "Ice Bucket Challenge" that swept the Internet in 2014 and raised more than $115 million for Lou Gehrig's disease (also known as amyotrophic lateral sclerosis or ALS) is an example of one success story (Rogers, 2016). Thanks in part to the funds raised by this effort, researchers discovered a new gene connected to the fatal disease. Lastly, social media can be a useful platform to engage policy makers in conversations about change, as well as to make them aware of (young) people's desire for that change.

In a study with US youth aged fourteen to twenty regarding how young people actually use technology to engage in civic issues, the majority of young people frequently use text messaging and email to communicate about opportunities for civic engagement, despite spending more of their time on Facebook in general (Farnham et al., 2013). However, youth with greater levels of experience with more public media platforms such as blogs or Twitter were also more likely to report higher levels of civic engagement in their communities. Participants with high levels of local community identification and civic self-efficacy (the notion that one can personally make a difference via civic engagement), along with public media experience (e.g., Twitter, blogging), were the most likely to be engaged in real-world civic engagement activities in their local communities.

For a sample of Malaysian and Indonesian youth aged fifteen to twenty-nine, Facebook was an important platform for participation in civic engagement (Warren, Jaafar, & Sulaiman, 2016). Participants from both countries reported using Facebook to both lend support to a cause and to connect with others who were motivated to address similar cultural issues. Overall, Malaysian participants reported using Facebook more often than their Indonesian peers to engage with civic issues. More specifically, Malaysian youth were more likely to use Facebook as a method to create awareness around social issues, to educate others, to organize in-person events in their communities, and to provide a space for debate compared to Indonesian youth. Achieving a more comprehensive understanding of social issues and accessing uncensored information was a benefit of Facebook endorsed by Malaysian youth, while Indonesian participants reported often turning to Facebook for news. Youth from both cultural contexts were least likely to use Facebook to engage with policy makers. This is not surprising given that both cultures are characterized by high power distance (which is associated with a respect for authority and hierarchy) and uncertainty avoidance (which translates as a level of discomfort with ambiguity; Hofstede, 2001; Warren et al., 2016).

Chinese youth aged fifteen to twenty-four reported mobilizing social media for similar purposes (Jiang & Kontauts, 2019). Discussion and information sharing (especially via videos) were among the most commonly cited reasons that Chinese adolescents shared for using social media with respect to civic participation. Inviting people to participate in in-person civic activities was the least commonly endorsed.

Despite the many ways that social media and technology help youth around the world to become more civically engaged, there are some challenges to that engagement. In some cases, the activism fostered by online networking and communication can put communities at odds with the government (UNICEF, 2017). This has led governments around the world to censor criticism of governmental views, policies, etc. In fact, about two-thirds of both adult and youth internet users live in countries that censor critical views (UNICEF, 2017). In addition, some youth do not recognize the utility of social media sites as platforms for social advocacy (UNICEF, 2017). Youth in Kenya have come up with a creative solution for the censorship problem (Mukhongo, 2014). Instead of posting their ideas and critiques using words (and consequently leaving little room for interpretation), youth reported using images and pictures to illustrate those sentiments instead. In some cases, young people do not want to address such "serious" issues when scrolling through their feeds on Facebook and Instagram, instead insisting that those sites should be reserved for recreation and having fun (Irannejad Bisafar et al., 2016). Sometimes adolescents also worry about how they will be judged by others after sharing their views online about social issues, which may make some adolescents reluctant to participate in public conversations online about those topics. As illustrated above, there are many advantages and avenues for youth civic engagement with the help of technology, but those benefits must be situated in cultural context. It also seems that the researchers have almost exclusively addressed these issues with older adolescents and emerging adults, suggesting that gleaning the perspective of younger adolescents with respect to technology and civic engagement would make a significant contribution to the literature. Furthermore, researchers may want to take a longitudinal approach to this topic to glean a richer understanding of developmental patterns with respect to how technology may promote civic engagement throughout adolescence and beyond. It would also be interesting to know more about the relations among activism, engagement, and adolescents' feelings of empowerment and desire to impart change in their communities in the future.

In considering the research reviewed above, it is clear that the benefits that technology access affords young people are diverse – spanning from improvement of health to the promotion of emotion regulation, identity development, and civic engagement. As increasing numbers of youth spend more and more of their time online, parents, educators, and teens themselves should be made aware of how that time could be spent most beneficially. Furthermore, a developmental perspective on these advantages is much needed, either throughout longitudinal research or through rigorous cross-sectional studies.

8 Hazards of Adolescent Technology and Media Use

"Sometimes I spend my time in front of [my] laptop from afternoon until night. I really would like to change my bad habit." Annisa, sixteen, from Indonesia (Kimball, 2019, p. 330).

"I sleep with my cell phone under my pillow." Sofia, pseudonym for a seventeen-year-old Guatemalan girl.

In *13 Reasons Why*, a series created and released by the popular online video streaming service Netflix, the viewer is given an intimate look at the events that led US high school student Hannah Baker to take her own life. Hannah records a series of cassette tapes describing the thirteen reasons that she chose to end her own life. Posthumously, those tapes are delivered to those individuals who played a key role in her life and, ultimately, in her decision to end it. The series debuted on March 31, 2017, and many appreciated the thoughtful attention being paid to such an important and timely topic – adolescent mental health – in hopes that the series would bring attention to increasing suicide rates among youth in the minority world.

However, researchers tracking monthly suicide rates in the USA against a control pattern of homicide rates reported a disturbing pattern (Bridge et al., in press). Unfortunately, the suicide rates among thirteen- to seventeen-year-olds increased in April 2017 above and beyond the predicted rate; this was the month immediately following the release of *13 Reasons Why*. More specifically, this increase resulted in 195 additional deaths from adolescent suicide beyond what would have been predicted when taking other factors into account. This increased pattern held true only for boys. Because celebrity deaths typically influence those who most identify with the deceased, the finding that girls' suicide rates were not adversely affected by the release of *13 Reasons Why* was unexpected. Perhaps the number of suicide attempts increased for girls following the series' release, but those data were not available for analysis.

In response to these troubling findings, the authors encouraged media professionals to approach topics like adolescent suicide with caution, living by the medical mantra "first do no harm." For example, Bridge et al. (in press) noted that portraying an adolescent struggling with suicidal ideation and then receiving support for those struggles would probably do more to address the stigma surrounding mental health than a suicide attempt that results in an adolescent's death. In other words, they argue that media professionals have a responsibility to reduce the likelihood of copycat episodes by thoughtfully addressing sensitive issues and considering the ways in which the events portrayed on screen may be interpreted by young viewers.

Professional organizations like the American Psychiatric Association have also raised important questions of how the media should address sensitive and timely topics like suicide (American Psychiatric Association, 2017). Their central concern is that in shows like *13 Reasons Why* complicated issues are addressed and handled (which is good for reducing stigma) without necessarily providing examples of how one should handle such situations. In response to the series, the American Psychiatric Association has compiled a comprehensive and approachable list of responses to common questions around mental health and suicide.

Although the above examples suggest that teens engage in copycat risky behaviors on occasion, most young people do not. Additional research is needed to identify the protective factors that prevent most teens from imitating the hazardous or deadly behaviors of media models.

Concern about the harmful effects of media on children and adolescents is not new. Cautionary messages about the negative effects of television and popular music on adolescents' emotions, aggression, and risky behaviors such as drug use and sexual behavior are widespread, as in this quote from the American

Academy of Pediatrics (2009, p. 1495), "Exposure to violence in media, including television, movies, music, and video games, represents a significant risk to the health of children and adolescents."

However, the notion that popular media directly imperils the well-being and behavior of teenagers is not supported by research. Almost all studies have been correlational rather than experimental, with little or no evidence for direct effects. The American Academy of Pediatrics (2009) report concludes that, "Research has associated exposure to media violence with a variety of physical and mental health problems for children and adolescents, including aggressive and violent behavior, bullying, desensitization to violence, fear, depression, nightmares, and sleep disturbances" (p. 1497). The key word in this quote is "associated," implying correlation rather than causation.

Consistent with a uses and gratifications approach, one early study of the lyrics of popular rock music revealed that only a minority of adolescents interpreted lyrics in the same way as adults did (Leming, 1987). In that study, adults concurred that the Olivia Newton John lyrics "Let's get physical" referred to an invitation to engage in sex, whereas only one-third of adolescents held that view, with the same percentage interpreting the lyrics as promoting exercise. Heavy metal music has been criticized for its themes of despair, rage, drugs, sex, rebellion, and greed. But in interviews, teenage boys who listened to heavy metal music reported that they often listened to the music when they were angry, but that the music dissipated their anger and calmed them down (Arnett, 1991). Those studies and others demonstrated that the users themselves are the experts on the motivations and consequences of media use. In general, research best supports the uses and gratifications theory of media – that individuals seek media that satisfy their social and psychological needs (Ruggiero, 2000). This approach recognizes the agency in adolescents' media choices and their appropriation of media inputs for their own purposes.

In looking at the use of "new" media or digital technologies by adolescents around the world, we need to keep in mind those lessons about correlation and lack of evidence for causation and direct effects. Adolescents are not passive recipients of technology; they select, adapt, and mold the ICT to suit their own purposes.

8.1 Internet Addiction

Gary and Jamie, two British adolescents, fit the profile of adolescents addicted to the Internet (Griffiths, 2000). Gary, fifteen years old, is proficient at programming and other digital skills. He sees his computer as his "friend" and has almost no offline social life. He suffers from a medical condition that further isolates him from others. His mother sees his excessive internet use as a vicious circle; his social awkwardness leads him to spend more time on the computer, and the time he spends on the Internet isolates him further from others. Jamie, a sixteen-year-old boy, spends approximately seventy hours per week on the Internet. He thinks about the Internet constantly, even when he is not online. Jamie reports that internet use can change his mood, either positively or negatively, implying that he is using media for coping and emotion regulation (Arnett, 1995). When Jamie is offline, he gets irritable and shaky. He reports that, "I can't work or live without it – my social and intellectual life are linked directly to it" (Griffiths, 2000, p. 213). Neither Gary nor Jamie saw his internet use as problematic or excessive. Although those extremes might be uncommon, it is clear that for some adolescents the Internet becomes an obsession, with clear withdrawal consequences when interrupted.

A recent ruling in China, the world's leader in revenue from online gaming, may be directed at teens like Gary and Jamie (Cheung, 2019). In late 2019, China announced that it would be enforcing a gaming curfew for adolescents related both to the amount of time that they are allowed to engage in online gaming each day and the amount of money they can spend monthly on online gaming sites. Gamers eighteen years old and younger are prohibited from playing online video games from ten p.m. to eight a.m.; their total time is limited to ninety minutes on weekdays and is extended to three hours on weekends and national holidays (Cheung, 2019). Time will tell about the effectiveness of this approach, but it certainly sends a message that young people should be spending much of their leisure time engaged in other activities.

Internet addiction among adolescents has been reported around the world, including among teenagers in Spain, Jordan, Norway, Turkey, China, Greece, Germany, Hong Kong, Taiwan, Korea, the UK, India, and Portugal. Internet Gaming Disorder (IGD) was added to the *Diagnostic and Statistical Manual for Mental Disorders-5* (DSM-5) as a topic that should be prioritized for future research (Rehbein et al., 2015), but internet addiction more broadly was not added as a disorder in the DSM-5. In May 2019, the World Health Organization also added a gaming disorder to the *International Classification of Diseases-11* (ICD-11; Gansner, 2019). The lack of a more general internet disorder addition to the DSM and the ICD may be because of continued debates about the definition of internet addiction and whether it is a single concept. As a result, many researchers are turning to the terms "problematic internet use" or "pathological internet use." One common definition of internet addiction is "compulsive behaviors related to any online activities that affect normal daily life and cause stress on social relationships" (Casaló & Escario, 2019, p. 344). Because there are no direct physical consequences of internet addiction as in alcohol or drug addiction, the definition relies on the social consequences. The primary theory that applies here is the displacement theory (e.g., Kraut et al., 1998). What would adolescents otherwise be doing if they were not using the Internet – interacting with family or friends, reading books or studying, engaging in sports or physical activity, or sleeping? Twenge and colleagues, for example, argue that time spent on the Internet is problematic when it interferes with sleep or with time spent in face-to-face interaction (Twenge et al., 2018). Other scholars argue that is the nature or quality of time spent on the Internet, especially using social media, that is critical rather than the amount of time (Marino, 2018).

Moreover, there may be cultural differences among definitions of internet addiction and what constitutes interference with normal daily life and social relationships. For example, Griffiths and colleagues suggest that the excessive concern about internet addiction in Korea and Taiwan stems from the fact that parents in those countries consider any time taken away from the family to be harmful (Griffiths et al., 2016). There are likely to be cultural differences as well with respect to acceptable peer and romantic relationships that may occur through social media.

A second issue in defining internet addiction is whether the addiction is to the Internet per se or to the activities performed on the Internet, for example, to gambling, pornography, shopping, or electronic gaming. As noted above, internet gaming disorder is a specific form of addiction that has been added to the addendum of the DSM-5 as deserving further study, suggesting that there is insufficient evidence at this time to add it as a diagnosis to the DSM-5 (Wichstrøm et al., 2019). Currently, experts tend to see a broad range of addictions, including those that employ the Internet as a medium as well as a specific addiction to internet use itself (Griffiths et al., 2016). Smart phone addiction is one subcategory of generalized addiction to the media. Although it has some features of internet addiction with respect to risk factors – personality traits and social environments – the factors are more similar to nonaddicted adolescents than to those with multiple media addictions (Jin Jeong, Suh, & Gweon, 2019). In other words, there are distinct features of addiction to a smart phone. The definitional complexity of internet addiction limits the generalizability of internet addiction studies.

Although there have been many studies of the factors associated with internet addiction, a meta-analysis by Fumero and colleagues best summarizes those findings (Fumero et al., 2018). The meta-analysis adopted PRISMA (Preferred Reporting Items for Systematic reviews and Meta-Analyses) criteria to identify and evaluate twenty-eight studies of problematic or excessive internet use. Most of the studies had been conducted in Asian countries. Findings showed that problematic internet use was associated with hostility, depression, and family difficulties. Protective factors showed smaller effect sizes but included self-esteem, social skills, and positive family relationships. The associations between internet addiction and personal and social factors, of course, are merely correlational and do not imply causation. Adolescents who are already depressed may be more inclined to use the Internet excessively or internet use may promote depression.

Studies of adolescents living in specific contexts reinforce those general findings and also introduce additional correlates of internet addiction. A 3-year longitudinal study of approximately 1,000 junior high school students from a rural region of Japan revealed relations between problematic internet use and a variety of psychological and physical problems (Kojima et al., 2019). Students who spent excessive time on the Internet were more likely to skip breakfast, go to sleep after midnight, experience sleepiness in the morning, and study for fewer hours. They also showed symptoms of depression. In addition, problematic internet use was associated with symptoms of the disorder orthostatic dysregulation or orthostatic intolerance. People with orthostatic dysregulation experience a variety of symptoms when standing up, including fainting; their symptoms are relieved when they recline. Disruptions in circadian rhythms may be provoked by late-night wakefulness and serve as a possible mechanism for development of the disorder.

8.2 Depression

Long hours spent on the Internet are likely to lead to depression in adolescents, according to Jean Twenge and her colleagues (Twenge et al., 2018). In a nationally representative sample of over half a million US adolescents, depressive symptoms and suicide rates rose during the years 2010 to 2015, especially among girls. During those same years, media use also increased, particularly the use of social media on the Internet and smart phones. There were significant correlations between screen time and psychological disorders, including depression and suicidal ideation. Adolescents who spent more time in face-to-face interactions, exercise or sports, homework, or attending religious services were less likely to report mental health problems. Economic factors were unrelated to teenagers' suicide rates and depressive symptoms. Twenge argues that increased screen time can increase feelings of loneliness and mental health symptoms. Although the US study revealed only correlations, she argues for a causal relation, citing a study by Kross et al. (2013) in which heavy Facebook use led to depression, but depression did not predict increased Facebook use among young adults.

Other studies have attempted to tease out the causal direction of the relation between heavy internet use and depression. A cross-lagged study of 1,715 Chinese adolescents revealed bidirectional effects that differed by gender (Liang et al., 2016). In boys, depression predicted later internet addiction; in girls, internet addiction predicted subsequent depression. The motivations for surfing the Internet also differed by gender, with girls more likely to seek information and boys more likely to seek entertainment. Findings continue to reflect the uses and gratifications model that individuals use media for their own purposes.

The heavy use of cell phones and texting may show patterns similar to internet use. In a six-year longitudinal study of texting among US adolescents, those with consistently high levels of texting (named perpetuals) experienced higher levels of depression, anxiety, and aggression and poorer relations with their fathers (Coyne, Padilla-Walker, & Holmgren, 2018). However, a sequential pattern of psychological symptoms and cell phone texting was not clear; the findings indicated only a relation among the variables. However, a cross-lagged study among 1,877 Korean adolescents revealed bidirectional effects of mobile phone addiction and depression. Heavy phone use predicted later depression and depression predicted excessive use of mobile phones (Jun, 2016). In sum, the relation between adolescents' excessive internet or cell phone use and depression appears to be consistent across cultures and genders. The relation may be bidirectional and appears to differ between boys and girls.

8.3 Cyberbullying

As indicated by the Pew Research Center with US youth, adolescents rated cyberbullying as the number one negative consequence of social media use (Anderson & Jiang, 2018). Research indicates that cyberbullying should be taken seriously, as it is associated with more serious mental health issues; in a study with nearly 2,000 US middle school students, those who had been either a perpetrator or a victim of cyberbullying were more likely to report suicidal ideation and to attempt suicide compared to peers not exposed to cyberbullying (Hinduja & Patchin, 2010). What exactly do we mean by cyberbullying? Defined by the Cyberbullying Research Center (2019), cyberbullying is the "willful and repeated harm inflicted through the use of computers, cell phones, and other electronic devices" (p. 2). It can be executed in a variety of forms, including making fun of others online or harassing someone via text message or email. The term cyberbullying relates both to the experience of being bullied (cybervictimization) and to the experience of bullying others (cyberaggression). Cyberbullies are more likely to also be cybervictims (Moreno-Ruiz, Martínez-Ferrer, & García-Bacete, 2019). As indicated by the findings described below, cultural context should be considered when exploring how cyberbullying shapes the lives of the world's youth. For example, in a sample of Spanish and Colombian adolescents, the risk factors for cyberaggression are best understood in light of a generally collectivistic and restrictive Colombian culture (Romera et al., 2017). In contrast, risk factors for cyberaggression in Spanish youth should be addressed through the lens of status and how the adolescents are perceived by their peers.

Estimates of cybervictimization vary widely and range anywhere from 10 percent to more than 40 percent of adolescents who report having experienced cyberbullying at some point in their lives (Cyberbullying Research Center, 2019). Some experts consider cyberbullying a public health concern, arguing that it increases the number of youth vulnerable to peer victimization (David-Ferdon & Hertz, 2007). More specifically, some youth will experience cyberbullying who would not otherwise be subject to peer victimization; only 36 percent of US adolescents who experience cyberbullying also experience harassment at school (Ybarra, Diener-West, & Leaf, 2010). Furthermore, cyberbullying allows the perpetrators to continue the harassment of their victims at home, meaning that the victimization can extend beyond the school day.

The likelihood of experiencing cyberbullying (as an aggressor and/or a victim) may be related to the adolescent's motivation for using social media (Young, Len-Ríos, & Young, 2017). For example, US adolescents who reported using social media for romantic reasons and who engaged in social comparison (i.e., the practice of measuring one's worthiness against others' successes) with their social media use were more likely to both be a victim and a perpetrator of cyberbullying. Social comparison was particularly problematic for girls in that girls who engaged in social comparison via social media use were particularly likely to experience cyberbullying. Those who reported using social media as a way to "belong" were more likely to be victims of cyberbullying. By comparison, adolescents who cited information-gathering or entertainment as primary reasons for using social media were less likely to be cyberbullies and cybervictims. These findings suggest that the tendency to experience cyberbullying is about more than just the amount of time that young people spend on social media. In other words, their reasons for using such SNSs may be related to their experiences with cyberbullying.

Perhaps the central concern regarding adolescents' experiences with cyberbullying is that being harassed is often associated with negative mental health outcomes like anxiety and depression. For example, depression was related to cybervictimization among Israeli youth (Ophir, Asterhan, & Schwarz, 2019). An analysis of adolescents' Facebook posts revealed that adolescents' explicit messages of distress shared on Facebook were associated with higher rates of self-reported depression. It is important to note that those messages were quite rare, though, as only 12 percent of participants shared such thoughts on Facebook.

In a sample of Chinese early adolescents, being cyberbullied was associated with feelings of anxiety and depression. That relation was partially mediated by adolescents' feelings of hopelessness (Chu et al., 2018). Self-compassion also played a moderating role. For those adolescents with low self-compassion, the relation between cybervictimization and anxiety and depression was much stronger.

In addition, much of the international research on cyberbullying during adolescence has focused on families and parenting. One study with Spanish youth addressed the relation between cyberbullying and Baumrind's parenting styles (Moreno-Ruiz et al., 2019). Adolescents raised in permissive (i.e., low on control and high on warmth) and authoritative (i.e., high on control and on warmth) households were less likely to report being cyberbullies compared to peers parented with authoritarian (i.e., high on control and low on warmth) and neglectful (i.e., low on warmth and on control) parenting styles. With respect to cybervictimization, adolescents raised by authoritarian parents were more likely to report being bullied online than peers raised in authoritative, permissive, or neglectful households.

Moreno-Ruiz et al.'s (2019) findings also revealed gender and age differences. Girls were more likely than boys to report being victims of cyberaggression, while the opposite gender pattern was reported for perpetrating cyberaggression. Adolescent girls raised by authoritarian parents were particularly vulnerable to the victimization of cyberbullying. Boys raised by permissive parents were more likely than boys raised in neglectful households or girls in authoritative ones to identify as cyberbullying victims. Lastly, older adolescents (youth aged fifteen to eighteen) were more likely to report being cyberbullies than younger adolescents (youth aged twelve to fourteen).

In a Costa Rican study, only 15 percent of middle adolescents (aged thirteen through seventeen) reported having been treated in an offensive or disagreeable manner in the past year and only 10 percent reported treating others in such a way (Pérez Sánchez, 2019). Most often the perpetrator of cyberbullying was from the same school, suggesting that the use of technology was associated with in-person bullying. Fewer adolescents reported being discriminated against online, and the great majority of those said that it was because they were not sufficiently feminine, suggesting that the root problem was sexism against girls (Pérez Sánchez, 2019).

Two studies – one with Chinese youth and another with Portuguese youth – highlighted additional risk and protective factors for cybervictimization

(Martins et al., 2016; Wang et al., 2019). Research from Wang et al.'s (2019) investigation with Chinese adolescents extended our knowledge regarding the cycle of violence in the relation between childhood maltreatment and the adolescent's likelihood of perpetuating cyberaggression. In short, childhood maltreatment did positively predict adolescent rates of cyberaggression. That relationship was mediated by adolescents' own moral disengagement. In other words, maltreatment during childhood made it more likely for adolescents to morally disengage; those youth found more hostile or aggressive responses to situations to be acceptable (Wang et al., 2019). Moral disengagement predicted higher rates of cyberaggression, probably because maltreated youth are more likely to find aggressive responses to situations to be acceptable. It is important to consider the cultural context as well. Abusive behaviors from Chinese parents directed toward their children are viewed as more acceptable than in other contexts and considered part of the parenting process. The value of filial piety (i.e., children's duty to take care of their parents) has been used as rationale for the justification of abusive behaviors (Wang et al., 2019).

In a cross-cultural study with Chinese and US adolescents, researchers compared the role of parents', teachers', and friends' intervention regarding adolescents' technology use and the propensity for cybervictimization (Wright, 2015). For all youth, regardless of culture, parental involvement in adolescents' technology use meant a strong and negative correlation between cybervictimization and depression and cybervictimization and anxiety. This finding suggests that the presence of parents in adolescents' lives may help reduce the negative psychological outcomes of cyberaggression. Patterns diverged culturally for the role of teachers and friends regarding technology use. For Chinese youth, teacher involvement with technology use was associated with stronger and more negative correlations between cybervictimization and depression and cybervictimization and anxiety. A similar pattern was revealed for US adolescents regarding friends' intervention with technology and the relation between cyberbullying and depression and cyberbullying and anxiety. These moderators point to important values in Chinese and US culture. The respect for elders makes teachers' involvement especially protective for Chinese youth, while the emphasis placed on peer culture in the USA made friends' involvement particularly beneficial for US adolescents.

In conclusion, these studies have provided us with some key pieces of information regarding both protective and risk factors of cybervictimization and cyberaggression. Furthermore, there is some support for the view that culture plays a central role in how cyberbullying is experienced by adolescents and how it may be prevented. Although the findings reported above provide important insights for parents and educators as they work to ensure adolescents' safety online, the results are correlational in nature. Thus future experimental studies with a control group should be a priority for investigators. Adolescents' insights and experiences from a variety of cultural contexts should also be systematically solicited in future studies. Having open conversations about the advantages and disadvantages of social media use with adolescents may be helpful in encouraging teens to set boundaries and realistic expectations for their social media use. Furthermore, continuing to check in with adolescents and providing social support could also help to mitigate the risk of negative mental health outcomes.

8.4 Eating Disorders

"I would like to be thinner, but that is not always possible . . . I get teased quite a lot in school. I'm changing school anyway because of that. 'Cause I just get picked on for being me." (Twelve-year-old British girl; Krayer, Ingledew, & Iphofen, 2007, p. 896)

"I know I am fat, but I like that, it doesn't bother me, I can wear what I want to wear and I've got good friends." (Australian high school girl; McCabe, Ricciardelli, & Ridge, 2006, p. 412).

Many adolescents, especially girls, engage in what Mimi Nichter calls "fat talk" (Nichter, 2009). The two quotes show distinct positions about body shape and thinness, although both girls are aware of the existence of the thin ideal. Fat talk, and its recognition of the thin ideal, may predispose adolescents to eating disorders. Eating disorders, including anorexia nervosa, bulimia nervosa, and binge-eating disorder, are more prevalent among adolescents than any other age group (American Psychiatric Association, 2015).

The centrality of media use in eating disorders became evident early in the study of those disorders (Harrison & Cantor, 1997; Stice et al., 1994). "The mass media [are] the most powerful means by which sociocultural ideals about beauty and body size are relayed to society" (Hood, Vander Wal, & Gibbons, 2009, p. 277). Mass media promulgate unrealistic images of female beauty, particularly the thin ideal. The dual pathway model of eating disorders (Stice & Bearman, 2001) suggests a pathway in which perceived cultural pressure to be thin, along with internalization of the thin ideal, leads to body dissatisfaction that promotes disordered eating. Once thought to be limited to the minority world, it is clear that eating disorders, like the media, have permeated the majority world as well (Bennett et al., 2004; Vander Wal, Gibbons, & Grazioso, 2008). For example, symptoms of eating disorders among young adolescent girls in Guatemala were comparable for all socio-economic groups and as high as those seen in minority world countries such as the USA (Vander Wal et al., 2008)

Arguably one of the most pernicious uses of the Internet is for mutual support among adolescent girls to foster their eating disorders, to attain and maintain an extremely thin unhealthy body weight. Websites named proana for proanorexia sprung up in the 1990s. In these "thinspiration" communities, girls shared photographs of emaciation and their strategies for achieving very thin bodies through food restriction and purging (Ging & Garvey, 2018. Quotes from proana sites include, "hunger hurts, but starvation works" and "hunger pains have become my latest addiction" (Ging & Garvey, 2018, p. 8). Attempts to shut down or ban such websites have not been entirely successful and instead the communities have gone underground with euphemistic tag names like "thigh-gap" or "size00" or have migrated to Instagram or Twitter (Arseniev-Koehler et al., 2016; Ging & Garvey, 2018). Although medical and psychological professionals are opposed to supporting eating disorders, some feminist researchers see value in the proana communities. They argue that the online spaces are safe sanctuaries for girls and offer support for resisting social pressures (e.g., Dias, 2003).

Because cultural pressures to be thin are often delivered through the media, many efforts to prevent eating disorders rely on increasing media literacy. For example, a summary of the programs aimed at preventing eating disorders revealed that a focus on media literacy, especially the ability to critique media ideals as well as to appreciate one's own body, were effective in preventing eating disorders (Levine & Smolak, 2016). An experimental study in which adolescent girls were exposed to thin-ideal media revealed similar findings (McLean, Paxton, & Wertheim, 2016). Media literacy mitigated the effects of thin-ideal exposure.

In sum, the media, and specifically the promotion of a thin body as the ideal female form, create the conditions for eating disorders for adolescent girls around the world. As a consequence, the most effective interventions for the prevention of eating disorders are based on critical media literacy, promoting adolescents' ability to critically examine media messages (Vander Wal et al., 2008).

8.5 Sleep Disturbances

Adolescents are at high risk of sleep disorders and sleep deprivation. Compared to younger children and adults, they experience a sleep phase delay: Their preferred sleep pattern is to stay up late and arise later in the morning (Exelmans & Van den Bulck, 2019). Yet the school day usually starts early; the result is often sleep deprivation and resulting declines in school performance. This confluence of physiological and social factors has been termed "the perfect storm" for adolescent sleep difficulties (Crowley et al., 2018).

Many adolescents report poor sleep quality and inadequate quantity. Studies show that excessive use of electronic media such as cell phones, tablets, and computers, especially near bedtime, can instigate or exacerbate sleep disturbances. Most of the studies are correlational and rely on self-reporting. A study from Norway is typical (Hysing et al., 2015). In a representative sample of 10,000 adolescents aged 16 to 19, sleep duration, the latency of sleep onset, and waking after first falling asleep were all related to the use of electronic devices at bedtime and the duration of electronics use during leisure time. Specifically, adolescents who used digital devices during their leisure time and at bed time slept less, took longer to fall asleep, and were more likely to wake up during the night. Similar findings emerged from a study of adolescents in Sweden (Jakobsson et al., 2019). Technology use near bedtime was associated with shorter sleep duration. Sleep difficulties were associated with stress at school and negative self-perception. A study of seventeen- and eighteen-year-olds in Spain also demonstrated an association between problematic phone use and duration of tablet use with self-reported and physiological measures of sleep difficulties (Cabré-Riera et al., 2019). In a study of over 40,000 children and teenagers in the USA, use of portable electronic devices was negatively related to sleep duration, and the relation was stronger for adolescents than for children (Twenge, Hisler, & Krizan, 2019). Young adolescents in the UK showed a similar negative correlation between use of electronic devices and sleep duration when the devices were used at night-time (Mireku et al., 2019). A mediation study of young adolescents in twelve countries revealed that sleep quality mediated the relation between screen time and psychological disorders as well as between school pressure and psychological disorders (Vandendriessche et al., 2019).

Despite the consistent findings for early, middle, and late adolescents of different countries, those studies are exclusively correlational. Therefore, it is impossible to know whether the use of digital media leads to sleep problems or whether adolescents with sleep difficulties choose to surf the web or use other digital media more extensively. Or perhaps there is a third, unknown variable such as an environmental or personality factor that affects both sleep and media use.

Most of the experimental studies of the effects of use of electronic media on sleep have been conducted with adults rather than teenagers. In one experimental study, young adults read an e-book or a print book for four hours before bedtime under dim light conditions. The digital media led to reduced levels of melatonin, an average of ten minutes longer to fall asleep, less REM (rapid eye movement) sleep, and decreased sleepiness according to self-reports (Chang et al., 2015). Readers of the e-book also felt sleepier the next morning. The light from the e-book contained more wavelengths in the blue range than the reflected light from the print book, and the authors suggest that the blue light suppressed melatonin production and led to a shift in the circadian rhythm. In another experimental study, adolescent boys wore either clear glasses or glasses that filtered out blue-wavelength light while using LED screens (Van der Lely et al., 2015). Compared to those who wore the clear lenses, those who wore the filtered glasses showed decreased alertness and less melatonin suppression. The physiological measures of sleep were not modified, although the duration of the screen use was not so long as in the previous study. Other studies suggest that short-duration use of devices emitting blue light might have minimal effects (Heath et al., 2014).

The proposed mechanisms for the sleep disturbances associated with the use of electronic media include: (1) displacement, (2) the effects of blue light on melatonin, and (3) general arousing effects of the media, especially gaming (LeBourgeois et al., 2017). It is likely that smart phone and internet use do displace sleep for some youth. The effects of blue light on melatonin are well established. Moreover, at least some activities, such as playing video games, may produce arousal that interferes with sleep (King et al., 2013; Weaver et al., 2010). Overall, the research findings imply that adolescents' use of digital media in the evening hours may have detrimental consequences for sleep, academic achievement, and overall health.

8.6 Violent Video Games

Does playing violent video games increase aggression? This has been one of the mostly widely studied issues in the field of media and behavior. A recent update of previous meta-analyses concludes that there is strong evidence for an effect. The answer is unequivocally "yes." Playing violent video games increases aggressive behavior, cognitions, and feelings and reduces empathy (Calvert et al., 2017). The effect occurs for older children, adolescents, and adults. The measures of aggressive behavior included "the administration of hot sauce or a noise blast to a confederate, self-report questionnaires, peer nomination and teacher rating of aggressiveness" (Calvert et al., 2017, p. 133).

There are still some unanswered questions, however. Does the content of the video games make a difference (for example, are cartoon figures less potent models for aggression than are actual people)? Although boys play video games more than do girls, is the effect on aggression similar across genders? Many studies have included only male participants. Because almost all research on this issue was done in minority world countries, do these findings hold for the majority world? Finally, there is a hypothesis that it is the competition inherent in video games that provokes aggression rather than the depiction of violence (e.g., Adachi & Willoughby, 2011). The resolution of these issues requires further investigation.

Beyond their effects on aggression, video games may confer benefits for adolescents. A meta-analysis revealed enhanced visuospatial cognition (Ferguson, 2007). There is evidence as well that playing prosocial video games can promote the development of empathy and prosocial behavior (Harrington & O'Connell, 2016).

8.7 Recruitment by Sexual Predators

"I was on Facebook, a guy asked me if I was a virgin, and if I wanted to have sex. Also, this guy asked me to send a picture of my breast, and this really bothered me." – Girl, fourteen. "Sort of like a chat room the person asked a question. Asked if you moon me would you have sex with me. Don't know if it was male or female that sent it." – Boy, sixteen. (Mitchell et al., 2014, p. 4)

One of the greatest fears of parents is that their children will be approached, groomed, and solicited for sexual or terrorist activity through the Internet. That fear is not unfounded, although many argue that the "technopanic" is unwarranted and stimulated by frightening news stories (e.g., Marwick, 2008). Although the numbers vary widely, up to 40 percent of teenagers have engaged in chatroom conversations of a sexual nature and up to 20 percent have received sexual solicitations, although most of those were not from adults but from other teenagers (Dombrowski et al., 2004; San Clemente & Cote, 2018; Wolak et al., 2008). Developmental factors may make adolescents particularly vulnerable to sexual predators; those include an emerging sexuality, a propensity for risk-taking, and interest in identity exploration. The features of the Internet – that it can be used anonymously and in isolated situations – also set the stage for sexual solicitation. The disinhibition effect – the tendency for individuals to self-disclose more online than in face-to-face interactions – may also play a role (Suler, 2004). Concerns about sexual predators have been raised not only in the minority world but in majority world countries such as Malaysia and Bangladesh (Shamim, 2017; Shukor et al., 2017).

The process of sexual solicitation of minors on the Internet starts with an introduction, usually in a chat room (DeHart et al., 2017). Surprisingly, most adult predators reveal their age rather than posing as adolescents. The next stage is grooming, forming a connection through discussing mutual interests, flattery, use of youthful internet terms, and introduction of sex talk. In the third stage the predator attempts to schedule a meeting (Olson et al., 2007).

Although many programs aimed at curtailing sexual solicitation on the Internet are aimed at parents, a receptive audience, an American Psychological Association report recommended addressing adolescents themselves (Wolak et al., 2008). Adolescents who are most vulnerable to sexual solicitation may be alienated from their parents or at least unresponsive to parental admonitions. The messages should be developmentally appropriate, acknowledging adolescents' interests in romance and sexuality. At the date of the report, 2008, there were few programs of that nature. A recent report summarizing programs to prevent risky behavior in adolescents did not specifically mention the inclusion of developmentally appropriate discussion of sexuality and romance but instead emphasized placing emphasis on possible negative outcomes and promoting appropriate social interaction (San Clemente & Cote, 2018). Therefore, this may continue to be a gap in the protection of adolescents from recruitment by sexual predators.

Of course, social media also have potential as agents of advocacy and awareness around sexual harassment – most recently through the #MeToo movement that launched in October 2017 in the United States after a host of allegations were made against Hollywood mogul Harvey Weinstein. It did not take long for the movement to become global (Adam & Booth, 2018). Although the campaign initially seemed to be aimed at adults, it quickly resonated with young people in the USA (Lu, 2018). The short hashtag that serves as a sign that one has been sexually abused or harassed has also been instrumental in giving teens an opportunity to speak out about their own experiences and to advocate for change (Lu, 2018). Teens have used the platform to not only share their own stories as victims of sexual misconduct but to address the role of societal gender norms. Such conversations have also raised awareness of K-12 educators in the USA, namely to promote children's agency in deciding how they want to interact with others (e.g., giving a "high five" instead of a hug). Given the recency of the #MeToo campaign, there is little empirical work in the social sciences on its impact, especially for teens. However, one potential intervention is to introduce the #MeToo issue in young adult literature and use those books as a starting point for discussion (J. Jacobs, 2018). Additional research is needed to understand the long-term impact of the #MeToo movement on teens in the USA and around the world.

8.8 Recruitment by Terrorists

As we were writing this Element about adolescents and technology, as a member of the board of a school in rural Guatemala, I (Judith Gibbons) received an official notice from Guatemala's Ministry of Education. The memo warned school administrators, parents, and teachers of two internet "games" identified by INTERPOL as being used by terrorists to solicit the help of adolescents in terrorist activities. The newest, named *Attack on the City*, simulates terrorist attacks by a lone wolf through the use of an automobile. The older game is called *Statement by Students in the Islamic State*. The Ministry advised parents and teachers to closely monitor the use of the Internet by their adolescent children and students.

Although there is almost no research on the recruitment of adolescents by terrorist groups, it is clear that terrorist groups such as ISIS are exploiting media use for their own ends (Al-Rawi, 2018). One video game designed and disseminated by ISIS followers, *The Clanging of the Swords*, is an adaptation of the well-known game *Grand Theft Auto*. The cover implies that "the types of real armed confrontations ISIS is engaged with are similar to the virtual wars produced in Western video games" (Al-Rawi, 2018, p. 746). An analysis of the comments on clips of the game revealed that about one-third of the comments were positive (Al-Rawi, 2018). These findings imply that further research is necessary on the influence of terrorist-inspired video games on adolescents around the world. Are terrorists achieving their mission?

8.9 Summary of Negative Consequences of Digital Media

Despite the many benefits of ICT use among adolescents, it is clear that digital media, especially the Internet, also confer risks. Those risks range from exposure to cyberbullying or recruitment by sexual predators or terrorists to the risk of addiction and sleep disturbances. Some parents, as well as investigators, have asked whether the overall impact of ICT on adolescents' well-being is positive or negative. In a time-use diary study of over 17,000 adolescents from 3 countries (Ireland, the USA, and the UK), screen time was unrelated to adolescent well-being (Orben & Przybylski, 2019). Further studies are needed to find out whether this finding holds for majority world countries.

9 Complex Effects of Media and Technology on Adolescents

Although some aspects of adolescents' media and technology use clearly yield only benefits or heightened risk for adolescent development, other aspects of young people's interaction with technology are more complex. For example, some domains can bring about advantages in some cases and elevate the potential for risk in others. In particular, we will highlight four of those complex areas – education, family, romantic relationships, and parasocial relationships – describing how the literature reveals advantages and disadvantages regarding the intersection of education, family, romantic relationships, and parasocial relationships with adolescents' technology and media use.

9.1 Education

The role of technology in education has been at the forefront of the discussion of how technology affects youth for several decades; questions around the role of technology in education gained strength after Prensky's (2001) concept of digital natives (explained in Section 3) encouraged teachers to consider educational and pedagogical changes in light of a new generation of learners. As with RACHEL, technology can improve access to educational resources at a low cost in communities in which such material would not otherwise be available (UNICEF, 2017). MOOCs (massive open online courses) have been widely touted as one means to close the access gap given that MOOCs carry no tuition fees, and many have been developed by professors at top US universities like Harvard and Stanford. However, a central challenge with MOOCs is that although enrollment is high, few students actually complete the course and few may be targeted specifically at adolescent learners (Clow, 2013).

Further advantages are that learning may be more enjoyable for students, more interactive, and more engaging because of the ways that technology can make learning relevant and relatable to students' everyday lives (UNICEF, 2017). Technology may also provide students with more opportunities for personalized learning in which students can enjoy and benefit from a more customized experience in which they acquire new knowledge and skills at their own pace (UNICEF, 2017).

Despite the justified critiques of Prensky's idea, the place of technology in adolescents' education remains a central one, but research has yielded mixed findings (Owston, 1997; UNESCO, 2011). For example, a study in the USA suggested that the presence of computers in schools was associated with higher test scores for students (National Center for Educational Statistics, 2001a, 2001b), while researchers in Australia reported a null relation between those two variables (Banks, Cresswell, & Ainley, 2003). Regarding computer access in the home, in a multi-country study with both minority and majority world countries represented, those adolescents who had at-home computer access actually had lower reading and mathematics test scores than peers who could not access the computer at home (Fuchs & Woessmann, 2004). However, when the authors further assessed how students were engaging with computers at home, those students who had been using computers for educational activities did perform better than peers who did not enjoy at-home computer access.

Students who spent time gaming on their home computers, however, scored lower on assessments of reading and math compared to peers who were not able to use computers at home.

In a study with Israeli adolescents, researchers were able to learn about adolescents' own views regarding nonacademic ICT use. The participants shared that they were aware that using ICTs for nonacademic purposes (e.g., gaming, social networking) would probably be associated with lower levels of academic achievement in their peers (Saloman & Kolikant, 2016). And adolescents' ICT use for nonscholarly purposes was, in fact, associated with lower school performance. However, results were more nuanced when asking about how adolescents felt that nonacademic ICT use would relate to their *own* academic performance. Although average academic performers generally reported that reducing their nonacademic time would probably correspond with a boost in school performance, reactions from both above and below average academic performers did not always support that pattern. Of course, the displacement model applies here (Kraut et al., 1998). In other words, if adolescents spend more time online engaged in nonacademic activities or online before bedtime, there is less time left for studying or sleep.

After introducing mobile devices (iPads were the most commonly used device) as part of classroom learning in independent schools in Western Australia, teachers noted that student motivation increased and not only offered benefits related to educational content but also yielded organizational benefits (Pegrum, Oakley, & Faulkner, 2013). Teachers also remarked that the devices themselves were not so critical to students' learning as much as the ways in which the devices could facilitate learning. Additional evidence supported the claim that students' learning also improved after mobile devices were introduced into the classroom. Teachers noted a series of challenges regarding the integration of mobile devices into classroom learning and mentioned that the technology that they had available to them was more beneficial for younger students compared to learners in the upper grades. Teachers commonly referenced challenges such as trouble with the devices themselves (i.e., with software and hardware) and ethical issues regarding students' use of the devices for appropriate purposes. Digital applications that allowed students to practice using a word processor and create spreadsheets and digital presentations were most useful for middle and high school students.

Approximately 50 percent of British university students reported using their personal smart phone for at least one educational purpose and more than 75 percent said they would be willing to do so if it would promote their learning (Woodcock, Middleton, & Nortcliffe, 2012). Among the most common uses were: applications to facilitate their school work (e.g., university-specific

Figure 9.1 Thirteen-year-old brother and sister from the USA use their cell phones for homework.

learning systems like Blackboard, communicating for group work), an internet browser for research, office productivity applications (e.g., word processors), and subject-specific tools (e.g., translators for foreign language courses and applications to track changes in the stock market). Challenges for students came primarily in the size of the smart phones themselves (the screen size is smaller than that of a tablet or computer) as well as limited battery life. Participants also noted that some applications were expensive, as most students were not willing to pay more than £5 for a single app. Two important issues to note here are that the students personally owned the devices and, as university students, were presumably developmentally equipped to assume responsibility for the role of technology in their own learning and to filter out the distractions that come along with using mobile phones for educational purposes.

As many teachers and professors know, cell phones can also present a significant distraction in the classroom. In a qualitative study with US secondary school students, most remarked that cell phones were a distraction during the school day (Tulane, Vaterlaus, & Beckert, 2017). For example, one student shared, "Texting distracts students from doing their work, even me. It takes our minds off of what we are learning" (Tulane et al., 2017, p. 719). Others felt that that by choosing texting over listening to teachers and engaging in the classroom, students were putting their social lives and reputation over their education:

If texting is not allowed, teachers have more of the students' attention and are able to teach them. If every other student was allowed to have their phone out to text anyone on their contact list, then they would be getting an A in their social lives, but an F in school. (Tulane et al., 2017, p. 719)

Interestingly, a few adolescents noted that they were using text messaging as a way to be *less* distracting; that is, they noted that it would be less distracting to text a friend or classmate as opposed to having a loud conversation with that person. Although this may be true, the practice seems to bring about some challenges for students' learning. Furthermore, despite Woodcock et al.'s (2012) promising data with respect to the use of cell phones to aid in learning at the university level, secondary students' accounts of distraction brought about by cell phones in the classroom suggests that cell phone use in high school classrooms with younger students, who have presumably less inhibitory control, should be undertaken with caution. In other words, children's and adolescents' developmental status should be taken into account when addressing the intersection of education and technology.

Many parents and educators around the world are also concerned about how adolescents' technology use at bedtime may be disruptive and how that may relate to academic performance (Arora et al., 2018). In a large sample of UK adolescents, engaging in social network use before bedtime was associated with lower grades in science and English, and mobile phone use prebedtime was associated with lower levels of academic performance in English and math. Video game use prior to bedtime was related to lower grades in English only. Video games were particularly problematic for adolescent boys' academic performance, while social networking and mobile phone use were particularly troublesome for girls. This study suggests that parents may need to be especially vigilant about monitoring their adolescents' technology use in the bedroom as bedtime approaches.

Of course, when considering issues of technology and education in the majority world, access to technology and the devices that afford that access must be considered. Furthermore, the learners most likely to benefit from technology in an educational setting are those who would not otherwise have the opportunity to pursue an education without technology. For example, girls in Afghanistan who are housebound because of local customs are building their reading skills through a text messaging program (Pence, 2015). In Bangladesh, videoconferencing is being used to connect urban teachers in Dakar with educators in more rural settings (UNICEF, 2017). The partnership allows the rural teachers in the low-resource schools to receive much-needed support and guidance from other educators. For fourth and fifth graders in rural India, some students living in villages so remote they are without electricity (solar panels were installed to allow the computers to function), the presence of computers in the classroom for students to use in small groups promoted advances in learning outcomes, but only when students reported high levels of computer self-efficacy (Ale, Loh, & Chib, 2017). Such a finding suggests that students must first perceive themselves to be competent with the devices in order for the technology to be a viable method to enhance learning.

These complex findings reveal that technology in educational contexts is not a simple "cure all." That is, the presence of computers and technology does not simply boost educational outcomes (UNICEF, 2017). Both students and teachers must be educated on how to use the technological resources available to them and troubleshoot challenges when they arise (Owston, 1997). Strong pedagogical frameworks must be a guiding force when integrating technology in the classroom. For example, the Organisation for Economic Co-operation and Development (OECD), based on data from more than sixty countries around the world, argued that technology in the classroom without pedagogy to support its use is without benefit (OECD, 2015). In order for students to use technology more efficiently in the classroom, the structure of the school day may need to be adjusted. Furthermore, access to computers and mobile devices should be monitored for a multitude of reasons as discussed above, but specifically in the context of educational uses of technology, parents and teachers should make sure that the adolescents stay on target and avoid distractions like gaming and excessive social media use.

9.2 Family

The role of technology and media in the family is complex. For example, adolescents (digital natives) often teach older family members (digital immigrants) how to navigate technology (social media in particular; Correa, 2016; Siibak & Tamme, 2013). Adolescents also shape how their families consume and use media. Thus the socialization norms around technology are somewhat different than in other domains, as youth are often the primary socialization agents for parents and grandparents with respect to technology. When referring to Chilean youth, Correa (2016) described adolescents as "agents of digital inclusion in the family" (p. 125). The young people in her sample were especially influential in shaping parents' ideas about computers and in-home internet access. This pattern was particularly characteristic of youth from low-income families compared to their higher-income peers. Researchers have also focused specifically on how families use ICT to communicate with one another (e.g., Tamme & Siibak, 2012). And, of course, there is also the issue of parental monitoring of children's ICT use and the level of restriction that parents place on their child's technology and media consumption (Symons et al., 2017). As noted above, parental monitoring may be especially necessary just prior to bedtime to ensure that young people are not overusing technology instead of sleeping.

Among middle-class urban families in India, changes in family dynamics due to the increase in cell phones have been dramatic. There were only 2.5 million smart phones in India in 2009 (of a population of about 1.3 billion), a number that increased to about 27 million in 2012 (Kapadia, 2017); that represents a 10-fold increase in only 3 years. Adolescents perceived cell phones positively; Rijuta, sixteen, said, "The cell phone is awesome! We use it for everything – staying in touch, planning what to do and where to meet, and of course, for talking with friends" (Kapadia, 2017, p. 122). A mother of a teenager saw them differently: "The cell phone is indeed a menace! It is very distracting for the adolescent" (Kapadia, 2017, p. 124). Although adolescents valued their independence in cell phone use, parents saw it as their responsibility to monitor their adolescent children's communication, leading to conflicts over privacy. The parenting model prevalent among urban families in India – that children are a project that parents must manage so that their children achieve success – probably exacerbates conflicts over cell phone use.

Social media sites like Facebook and videoconferencing and instant messaging services like Skype are used among generations to stay connected to one another despite geographic distance (Siibak & Tamme, 2013). As was the case in many three-generation Estonian families, the oldest generation said that they decided to engage with ICT because it allowed them to stay current with younger family members (Siibak & Tamme, 2013). Others used those tools as a way to plan time to see each other. In many cases, efficiency was cited as an important factor, especially when trying to coordinate plans with multiple extended family members simultaneously. It was even more common for family members living as a single household to use such technology for communication compared to family members living in separate cities. Participants reported using such tools to manage minor aspects of daily life like planning trips to the grocery store.

Although the ability to stay closely connected and "in the know" via Facebook boasted many benefits, sometimes members of the older generations reported being irritated or annoyed with the adolescents and emerging adults in light of the content that the young family members were sharing online. In other cases, it was the youngest members who were vexed by the social media presence of older family members. A twelve-year-old girl from the UK shared:

> [T]he boys in my class have taken to following my mum's Flickr [a photo sharing website] and then making fun of me at school. I once wrote an essay

in school that we had to post on a blog; I added a picture to the essay and, when you clicked on it, it took you to my mum's Flickr. Yes . . . and then they [the boys at school] photoshopped my pictures and posted them. (Siibak & Tamme, 2013, p. 82)

In a separate intergenerational study with Estonian families, ICT was again central for facilitating communication among the generations and was particularly beneficial when reinstating intergenerational conversations that may have lapsed due to physical distance or other factors (Tamme & Siibak, 2012). These ICT-fueled connections seem to be most beneficial for the eldest family members.

Regarding parental monitoring and guidelines of teens' technology use, qualitative findings from US parents revealed that it was difficult for some parents to simply accept the significant amount of time that many adolescents spend engaged with technological devices and on social media (Symons et al., 2017). Due to the pervasive nature of social media in many adolescents' lives, mothers and fathers were concerned that their adolescent children may have a difficult time discerning what should be kept private and what is acceptable to share publicly on social media. Furthermore, as a consequence of the importance of having a high status (i.e., having many friends and connections on social media), parents feared that adolescents would not engage in critical thinking when making online connections. In other words, they feared that adolescents would act solely to boost their online popularity.

Parents were also aware of the benefits their adolescent children enjoy from connectivity. Those benefits were mainly social in nature, but parents noted that technology access helps adolescents in academic endeavors as well. When asked specifically about how they view their role as monitors or gatekeepers of their children's online lives, most parents replied by saying that it is a good opportunity to afford their children some autonomy while maintaining oversight as necessary. In many parent-child teams, there was room for negotiation, as adolescents regularly requested more independence than parents were willing to give. Not surprisingly, there was also a developmental component of this negotiation; younger children were granted less autonomy than their older counterparts. This gradual granting of autonomy signaled trust in the parent-child relationship. Such negotiations speak to a more general issue for many of the world's parents and their adolescent children – the ever-present quest by adolescents to gain more freedom and independence and the parental task of balancing that need for growing autonomy with the parents' task of keeping the child safe and protected (Poelker et al., 2017).

Figure 9.2 A fifteen-year-old Guatemalan girl said, "I think technology is an incredibly important and useful part of life, but we need to be careful not to get addicted so we can live in the moment."

9.3 Romantic Relationships

Like communication among adolescents with their parents and other relatives, technology has shaped communication patterns between adolescent romantic partners, especially through the use of texting and Facebook (Baker & Carreño, 2016). ICT has become essential for adolescents' communication with their romantic partners for daily conversation (Subrahmanyam & Greenfield, 2008); mobile phones play a particularly important role (Stonard et al., 2017). British youth noted that, ideally, they would check in digitally (e.g., phone call, text message) with their romantic partner daily, but there are instances when the communication can become too frequent (Stonard et al., 2017). For example, a thirteen-year-old girl shared her views: "But urm, like you wouldn't want them to be like obsessive and not like every hour of every day that's just like stupid questions like how are you like over the day" (Stonard et al., 2017, p. 2093). Another girl added, "You can be like over obsessive like every minute hello hello hello hello hello hello and it just keeps going on" (Stonard et al., 2017, p. 2093). Thus because technology makes communication easier, there can be a tendency to become overly communicative or to develop an obsessive need to be in touch. Communication via text message also left some of the British adolescents, specifically girls, feeling anxious while waiting for a boyfriend's reply. Girls shared reports of friends repeatedly checking their phones. Others tried to disconnect by turning off their phones altogether and then eagerly expected to have a message waiting when they turned their phones on again. When girls attributed the lack of response to being ignored, it was particularly hurtful.

The role of technology appears to evolve over the course of the relationship; adolescent boys and girls may also view the role of technology in the relationship differently (Baker & Carreño, 2016). Girls in the USA found texting and Facebook helpful in getting to know their potential romantic partners before initiating a relationship. One adolescent girl explained, "We started talking on Facebook, and then we would text, and then it kind of just . . . grew. So, then we became boyfriend and girlfriend after like 3 months of talking" (Baker & Carreño, 2016, p. 312). Boys reported using social networking sites differently in the initial stages – primarily as a way to obtain a girl's phone number. Mexican American adolescent girls reported commonly using Facebook to flirt (Adams Rueda, Lindsay, & Williams, 2015). Belgian youth also suggested that social media could be useful in fostering a new romantic relationship (Van Ouytsel et al., 2015). For example, if an adolescent was romantically interested in a peer, they often "liked" that person's past posts or photos as a way to foster communication before officially beginning the relationship.

Once the relationship became "official," updating one's relationship status on social media was an important next step. That public milestone (known as becoming "Facebook official"), however, often brought challenges for the young couple, like jealousy, for example (Baker & Carreño, 2016; Adams Rueda et al., 2015). Sometimes other girls intervened by messaging another girl's boyfriend even though it was clear that that boy was already formally dating someone else. Girlfriends were also unhappy when boys kept photos of other girls on their cell phones or when other girls "liked" their boyfriend's photo or post on social media. One adolescent girl shared:

> Oh, insecurity. I guess when like they're talking to other girls or like they have girls' pictures and stuff on their phone. Like don't give a girl a reason to compare ourselves to another girl and bring down her self-esteem. (Baker & Carreño, 2016, p. 313)

From the adolescent boy's perspective, one boy noted, "My chick get mad though, when I Instagram. You know that's only pictures, yeah? And, then loads of girls like my pictures. And she get mad" (Baker & Carreño, 2016, p. 313). Overall, teens differed in their views on the extent to which they should use technology to "keep tabs" on their romantic partner. This issue of monitoring yielded diverse reactions from US participants, for example. Some adolescents (both boys and girls) felt that sharing passwords was particularly reasonable. Others mentioned that they monitored their partner's behavior because they wanted to make sure that they were safe, while others felt that the "checking in" was rooted in jealousy, as illustrated by the following girl's challenges with staying in touch with an ex-boyfriend while dating someone new:

> And, he [her new boyfriend] saw that we were friends and that we were still talking and he started going, "Why are you still friends with him [the ex-boyfriend]? Why are you still talking with him? You guys are over. You shouldn't be doing that." And, he actually asked for my password and username, logged in, and de-friended him. (Baker & Carreño, 2016, p. 315)

Checking social media activity online and reviewing text conversations on their partner's phones were common monitoring behaviors among adolescents in the UK (Stonard et al., 2017). The tendency to monitor was particularly common among girls. Work with Mexican American youth supported the conclusion that using ICT in relationships makes defining "cheating" more complicated, as simply corresponding with members of the opposite sex was viewed by some partners as cheating (Adams Rueda et al., 2015). For some adolescents from the UK, the monitoring behavior resulted in the end of a relationship:

> Yeah, it's like, I've had the experience where they've had no trust and they got my Facebook password and stuff because I trusted them but they didn't trust me and they dumped me because I was putting X's [kisses] to a female. (Stonard et al., 2017, pp. 2097–2098)

At the end of the relationship, US adolescents used technology to break up (Baker & Carreño, 2016). Using an indirect approach, they would delay answering text messages until they stopped responding altogether. In many cases, the relationships ended without any face-to-face discussion. In more direct break-ups, young people would end things via a phone call or text message and, rarely, via social media.

After the relationship ended, UK participants mentioned that sometimes abuse or harassment of the ex-partner continued (Stonard et al., 2017). Many adolescent boys thought that the hostility was less concerning when it was perpetrated virtually. A fifteen-year-old boy explained:

> It's just as simple as turning it off, like you don't have to look at the messages, it's not like face-to-face bullying where they are saying it and you can't get away from it or if they are physically hitting you and you can't get away from it. (Stonard et al., 2017, p. 2101)

A few adolescent girls remarked that the prevalence of ICT made break-ups more challenging, as there was the opportunity to stay in constant contact.

Belgian youth reported removing evidence of former romantic partners from their social media accounts by deleting photographs from their social media profiles (Van Ouytsel et al., 2015). Furthermore, copies of the messages were easily saved for repeated referencing. This seemed to intensify the harmful effects of such correspondence. That idea was illustrated by a fourteen-year-old girl: "It gets in your head and you can't get away from it because you want to keep reading over the conversation" (Stonard et al., 2017, p. 2103).

Mexican American youth echoed many of the same issues as noted above (Adams Rueda et al., 2015). For those adolescents with higher levels of acculturation, ICT was particularly central to their communication with romantic partners. One novel idea that emerged from those focus groups was that technology can be used by parents and/or peers to intervene in unhealthy relationships or violent situations. Adolescents often used Facebook to publicly share their relationship challenges – either because other adolescents referenced the fight itself or the negative feelings that followed were shared openly via social media status updates. Some adolescents also reported that their parents read their text messages directly. Because this finding emerged only in the study with Mexican American adolescents, perhaps there is a cultural element to the ways in which parents use technology to intervene on their adolescent child's behalf.

Research with Canadian youth examined the relation between internet use for different purposes and the quality of romantic relationships and friendships (Blais et al., 2008). The patterns were similar for friends and romantic partners. For example, using instant messaging was positively associated with romantic relationship and friendship quality one year later. Conversely, playing games on the Internet and using chat rooms were negatively associated with relationship quality – both romantic and friendship.

9.4 Parasocial Relationships

Parasocial relationships are best described as one-sided or unidirectional, as one member of the dyad does not know that the other exists (Tukachinsky & Dorros, 2018). For example, a teen becomes enthralled with a famous athlete or celebrity and becomes invested in the (imaginary) "relationship." Access to such well-known figures via the media (e.g., television, social media accounts like Twitter and Facebook) can allow teens to feel as though they "know" the other person. For example, "stories" on popular platforms like Instagram allow users to upload a series of images or short videos to provide followers with real-time updates regarding what the person is thinking about or doing at that particular moment. When viewing celebrities' Instagram stories, users can feel even more connected to the media figure. Twitter may also promote feelings of intimacy (Bond, 2016).

Often, these parasocial relationships are romantic in nature – akin to a "celebrity crush" – and are referred to as parasocial romantic relationships (PSRRs; Tukachinsky & Dorros, 2018). PSRRs provide a safe space for adolescents to experience romantic relationships without assuming the traditional risks (e.g., unsafe sexual behaviors, rejection; Erikson, Harrison, & Dal Cin, 2018). Fantasies are especially critical for the romantic component of some parasocial relationships and also provide young people with a safe space to explore their sexual identity and a space for adolescents to explore the ideal version of their self-concept. Erikson et al.'s (2018) four-part model of parasocial attachment displays adolescents' parasocial relationships as a precursor to the initial stages of Brown's (1999) romantic development theory. The four components include behaviors, cognitions, emotions, and fantasies. Emotionally, adolescents become attached to and invested in the lives of those with whom they have parasocial romantic relationships. They even report feeling empathy for the media figure. Cognitively, these relationships provide low-stakes opportunities to practice scripts and utilize schemas for romantic relationships. Parasocial relationships also provide adolescents with opportunities to address issues of identity development; more specifically, these relationships encourage adolescents to think about how they are alike and different from the media figures who they admire. In some cases, adolescents engage in particular behaviors to help them become closer to celebrities (e.g., waiting outside of a celebrity's favorite coffee shop for a chance to meet them). As Erikson et al. (2018) note, such topics are often the focus of clinical research on (pathological) fan behavior, but that view does not represent a comprehensive understanding of adolescents' parasocial relationships.

Although such imaginary relationships are often dismissed as childish or silly, some researchers have suggested that PSRRs play an important role in adolescents' identity development (Gleason, Theran, & Newberg, 2017) and could be related to their overall attachment patterns (Erikson et al., 2018). Before describing some of the findings associated with research on adolescents' parasocial relationships, it is important to note that this line of research has been conducted exclusively with US participants.

Adolescent boys and girls often differ with respect to the partner in the "imaginary" relationship (Gleason et al., 2017). Boys are more likely than girls, for example, to form parasocial relationships with athletes who served a mentoring role (as opposed to being a friend). Girls were more likely to choose actresses. Across both genders, adolescents chose celebrities who are known for their roles on television or in film (as opposed to celebrities who have made a name through other forms of media). It is critical to note that for 61 percent of the sample, the parasocial relationships were romantic. Those who reported the romantic component also indicated more intense emotional involvement with their parasocial partner compared with parasocial relationships that were platonic or hierarchical (e.g., mentor or authority figure) in nature. Adolescent boys and girls did not differ in the intensity of emotional involvement or the frequency with which they discussed their celebrity partners with their families. In prior research with emerging adults, however, women reported greater intensity in their parasocial relationships than men (e.g., Cohen, 2003), suggesting that these parasocial (romantic) relationships are best understood within a developmental framework.

In a study with US adolescents and university students (who provided retrospective data on former PSRRs), participants who engaged in PSRRs as adolescents reported more idealized romantic beliefs (Tukachinsky & Dorros, 2018). University student participants who had experienced more intense emotional involvement in their parasocial relationships as adolescents (e.g., imagining that their imaginary partner could be a true companion) reported lower levels of satisfaction in their current real-life romantic relationships compared to those with less intense emotions in their adolescent PSRRs. No significant patterns were found between physical attractiveness in PSRRs and current relationship satisfaction.

The complex relation between technology and adolescent development is nicely illustrated in a study with Italian youth (Borca et al., 2015). Focus group data with adolescent participants supported the notion that adolescents do use technology to feel close to peers, as exemplified by this quote from a tenth grade boy: "We mostly use apps like messenger to talk to friends, to meet and find out what to do" (Borca et al., 2015, p. 54). Italian teens' internet use also highlighted a source of tension with parents, especially with respect to navigating their technology and media use and adolescents' desired autonomy in this domain. An eighth grade girl shared, "I usually get on [the Internet] when my mom isn't there so I can stay on longer, because according to my mom I can only stay on for 30 minutes" (Borca et al., 2015, p. 54). A tenth grade boy provided a similar view: "They [his parents] don't like it because they say it wastes time" (Borca et al., 2015, p. 54). Thus ICT use as a source of conflict and an area of negotiation between parents and adolescents seems to be a shared experience for many of the world's youth (e.g., Borca et al., 2015; Symons et al., 2017). Participants' responses also strongly supported the notion that interaction with technology fosters their identity development, as the Internet helped participants feel connected to others and also stand out and establish their own independent sense of self.

Figure 9.3 RACHEL in use in a Guatemalan classroom.

In short, the role that technology plays in relationships – both interpersonal and parasocial – is not simple. On the one hand, ICT facilitates frequent communication with close others like grandparents and romantic partners. On the other, it exposes young people to the intimate details of celebrities' everyday lives, which may lead to parasocial relations. Such relationships are often the launching point for many important developmental processes. Furthermore, technology has significantly changed how adolescents communicate with peers and family members. It has introduced new challenges for adolescents and their parents concerning autonomy and altered the process of courtship for youth around the world, while providing adolescents with a space to develop their sense of self and pursue the central task of adolescents – identity development. The role that technology continues to play in adolescents' social and emotional development must remain a top priority for researchers around the world.

10 Conclusion

The means by which technology and media shape adolescents' lives around the world are complex. Although uses like entertainment and education quickly come to mind, the story is much more nuanced. Many of the ways in which adolescents consume media help young people complete the prominent developmental tasks of adolescence, including in the domains of cognition and socio-emotional development. As illustrated in this Element, young people use the Internet to explore their possible selves and engage with others in similar situations. Whether they be youth who identity as LGBTQ or immigrants to a new culture, young people have sought refuge online to cope and thrive in these situations as they grapple with their evolving sense of self. Staying connected online has also been essential for peer interactions, such as maintaining friendships and romantic relationships. In many ways, the basic nature of these interpersonal connections has been transformed due to the capability of always being in touch with one's friends and/or romantic partners via social media, texting, etc. Technology is sometimes used by youth to learn or practice skills needed for their future work. As described earlier, with the help of RACHEL, Guatemalan students will be able to make artisanal ice cream to sell at a local community gathering. Such activities prepare adolescents for future employment and provide a concrete example of how technology can inform (and improve) that work.

The specific advantages and disadvantages of adolescents' technology use are diverse, and many domains yield both positive and negative consequences. Positive consequences include an engaging delivery of health intervention content, a venue for honing emotion regulation and boosting empathy, the promotion of identity development, and encouraging civic engagement. Negative ones include concerns surrounding addiction, sleep disturbance, depression, eating disorders, and cyberbullying. Perhaps the impact of technology and media is best described as complex or a combination of both positive and negative consequences. Domains with more complex outcomes include education and familial, romantic, and parasocial relationships.

When interpreting the research conducted on adolescents' technology use and its impact on an international scale, it is essential to remember that the adolescents' settings, cultures, and economic resources impact their experiences with technology. As developmental psychologists, it is difficult for us imagine or discuss the use of technology in adolescents' lives without considering the role of culture. As described above, adolescents engage with media that fit their personal needs and interests, both of which are likely to be shaped by cultural context. Furthermore, if economic limitations prevent adolescents from consuming media or using technology at home, instead engaging with it only at school, the experiences of those youth are likely to be very different from those of their counterparts who own their own smart phones, tablets, and/or laptops.

Looking ahead, we cannot emphasize enough the importance of continued research at the intersection of technology and media with development. Moving forward, researchers should make a concerted effort to include more diverse samples from both the minority and the majority world. As described in this

Element, cultural context matters greatly in this area of research, and that diversity must be addressed in this area of research. An area in particular that could use immediate attention is the gathering of technology and media usage statistics for youth in majority world countries. Such basic information provides researchers, parents, and educators with important insights regarding how youth in that context consume media, which would provide an empirically based launching point for future studies.

Methodological diversity is also important. Quantitative questionnaires with only closed-ended questions are not likely to adequately capture the complexity or variability in how adolescents around the world use technology. For example, similar to the tours of their bedrooms provided by US teens, adolescents could be asked to provide a "tour" of their digital worlds. Participatory action research approaches should also be considered. In short, adolescents' voices and lived experiences must remain at the heart of this research to ensure that researchers are addressing the most pressing and current developmental issues in this domain.

One observation that we made when reviewing the literature for this Element is that few findings were interpreted in a cultural context. Although there were data collected from a variety of different countries, rarely were the findings interpreted through a cultural lens. In other words, researchers must go beyond mentioning the participants' nationality in the method section and work to interpret their findings through a cultural lens. An exception is a study on Mexican American adolescents' technology use in romantic relationships by Adams Rueda et al. (2015); those authors couched parental monitoring of an adolescent's technology use and occasional intervention should problems arise in light of values associated with Mexican culture.

Finally, in terms of future research, investigators should also prioritize longitudinal approaches. Longitudinal studies have long been considered the gold standard of research by developmental psychologists, but the need for a longitudinal perspective is especially central in this domain for two primary reasons. First, it provides researchers with information on the developmental patterns of technology use as adolescents move through their teen years. Seeing as the technological field is an ever-changing moving target, the field would benefit from an understanding of how the same young people navigate the changes and new developments in the field. Is their development impacted? What changes seem to be more beneficial? Which are more problematic? Second, it is important to gain a better understanding of how technology impacts communities over time and how those changes shape adolescents' lives. Take the RACHEL project as an example. Jackline and Mustapha in Tanzania and Ghana, respectively, reported immense excitement among students regarding the addition of RACHEL to their classrooms. Our conversations with the Guatemalan team, a group that has been using and benefiting from RACHEL for far longer, suggested that that initial enthusiasm does fade and adolescents do acclimatize to RACHEL's role in their school day. Even Jackline from Tanzania remarked that in the weeks following that initial wave of enthrallment with RACHEL's introduction to the school day, students had to be gently reprimanded for using tablets to take photos and make videos for fun instead of to learn. That longitudinal perspective would probably also reveal the "ripple effects" that adolescents' technology use and media consumption are having in the community as whole. Recall the youth in Ghana who worked to reduce standing water in their local community after learning via research with RACHEL that standing water is the perfect breeding ground for mosquitos.

In light of the research reviewed in this Element, we think that there are important recommendations for parents, teachers, and policy makers regarding adolescents' technology use. The application of the information reviewed here could help improve adolescents' daily lives in a variety of ways. Whether it be in the classroom or spending time with friends in the afternoon, the adults in adolescents' lives must be aware of the complex role that technology plays.

Parents should set clear guidelines for technology use. These expectations should address things like how much screen time adolescents are allowed in a day and the types of media that they are permitted to engage with on their devices. For example, in a family we know with four rising teenagers, the parents have set the following guidelines: the children will receive a phone on their thirteenth birthday, they are not allowed to download games except on one iPad that is shared among the four of them, and their electronic devices must be stored upstairs at night away from the children's bedrooms. Of course, the specific rules will vary from family to family, but some parameters should be in place. Once the guidelines are established, parents should view technology as a domain in which they can practice allowing adolescents some autonomy. Parents should also check in regularly with their adolescent children about their experiences with technology, focusing especially on social media use. These frequent conversations could help identify instances of cyberbullying and also convey to the adolescents that they can trust that their parents will be a source of support should the need arise.

Educators should not underestimate the critical role of pedagogy regarding technology use in the classroom. In other words, technology should not be incorporated blindly but should instead be integrated after careful planning. When designing opportunities to enhance classroom learning, teachers should pay close attention to the literature on the benefits of technology in education, such as allowing students a more personalized environment. One way to minimize the negatives like distraction would be to ask students to leave their cell phones at the door. Of course, this rule may not work well in settings in which a students' cell phones are their only means of accessing technology for learning, but in minority world contexts especially, where access to devices is not a common concern, this rule may be a simple way to improve the classroom environment. Like parents, teachers should also seek student feedback on the perceived advantages and disadvantages of having technology in the classroom. Such conversations also serve to promote adolescents' agency and help ensure that adolescents' experiences remain at the core of teachers' decision-making regarding how technology is used in the classroom.

Policy makers must consider that technology is not an immediate "cure" for all problems. It seems that technology is often proposed as a magic solution to all of the problems facing the world's youth. In many cases, access to technology and opportunities to promote digital literacy are beneficial for adolescents, but there are documented risks as well. Chile's recent restrictions on advertising unhealthy food in an effort to combat the country's obesity epidemic could provide one framework for government involvement (A. Jacobs, 2018). Perhaps one key next step would be to fund research that addresses the comprehensive experiences of technology use among teens – under what circumstances is technology use beneficial? Or harmful? Furthermore, how do cultural values, access to economic resources, age, etc. impact those consequences? Because of the ever-changing nature of the field, the government's role in addressing media-related issues in adolescents' lives must be constantly reevaluated. The need for researchers, parents, and educators to stay engaged in these conversation is also essential for the well-being of adolescents around the world.

References

Adachi, P. J. and Willoughby, T. (2011). The effect of video game competition and violence on aggressive behavior: Which characteristic has the greatest influence? *Psychology of Violence*, 1(4), 259. doi:10.1037/a00224908

Adam, K. and Booth, W. (2018, October). A year after it began, has #MeToo become a global movement? *The Washington Post*. Retrieved from https://www .washingtonpost.com/world/a-year-after-it-began-has-metoo-become-a-global-movement/2018/10/05/1fc0929e-c71a-11e8-9c0f-2ffaf6d422aa_story.html

Adams Rueda, H., Lindsay, M., and Williams, L. R. (2015). "She posted it on Facebook": Mexican American adolescents' experiences with technology and romantic relationships. *Journal of Adolescent Research*, 30, 419–445. doi:10.1177/074355841456236

Ale, K., Loh, Y. A.-C., and Chib, A. (2017). Contextualized-OLPD education project in rural India: Measuring learning impact and mediation of computer self-efficacy. *Educational Technology Research and Development*, 65, 769–794. doi:10.1007/s11423-017-9517-2

Al-Rawi, A. (2018) Video games, terrorism, and ISIS's Jihad 3.0. *Terrorism and Political Violence*, 30(4), 740–760. doi:10.1080/09546553.2016.1207633

American Academy of Pediatrics. (2009). *Policy Statement: Media Violence*. Retrieved from https://pediatrics.aappublications.org/content/pediatrics/124/ 5/1495.full.pdf

American Psychiatric Association. (2015). *Feeding and Eating Disorders: DSM-5 Selections*. Arlington, VA: American Psychiatric Association.

American Psychiatric Association. (2017). 13 mental health questions about "13 Reasons Why." Retrieved from https://www.psychiatry.org/news-room/apa-blogs/apa-blog/2017/04/13-mental-health-questions-about-13-reasons-why

Anderson, M. and Jiang, J. (2018). *Teens, Social Media and Technology 2018*. Retrieved from http://publicservicesalliance.org/wp-content/uploads/2018/ 06/Teens-Social-Media-Technology-2018-PEW.pdf

Anderson-Fye, E. P. (2003). Never leave yourself: Ethnopsychology as a mediator of psychological globalization among Belizean schoolgirls. *Ethos*, 31, 59–94. doi:10.1525/eth.2003.31.1.59

Apaolaza, V., Hartmann, P., Medina, E., Barrutia, J. E., and Echebarria, C. (2013). The relationship between socializing on the Spanish online networking site Tuenti and teenagers' subjective wellbeing: The role of self-esteem and loneliness. *Computers in Human Behavior*, 29, 1282–1289. doi:10.1016/ j.chb.2013.01.002

Appel, M. (2008). Fictional narratives cultivate just-world beliefs. *Journal of Communication*, 58, 62–83. doi:10.1111/j.1460-2466.2007.00374.x

Arnett, J. (1991). Adolescents and heavy metal music: From the mouths of metalheads. *Youth Society*, 23, 76–98. doi:10.1177/0044118X91023001004

Arnett, J. J. (1995). Adolescents' uses of media for self-socialization. *Journal of Youth and Adolescence*, 24(5), 519–533. doi:10.1007/BF01537054

Arnett, J. J. (1999). Adolescent storm and stress, reconsidered. *American Psychologist*, 54(5), 317–326. doi:10.1037/0003-066X.54.5.317

Arnett, J. J. (2010). *Adolescence and Emerging Adulthood: A Cultural Approach* (4th edition). Upper Saddle River, NJ: Prentice-Hall.

Arnett, J. J. (2012). *Adolescence and Emerging Adulthood: A Cultural Approach* (5th edition). Upper Saddle River, NJ: Prentice-Hall.

Arora, T., Albahri, A., Omar, O. M., Sharara, A., and Taheri, S. (2018). The prospective association between electronic device use before bedtime and academic attainment in adolescents. *Journal of Adolescent Health*, 63, 451–458. doi:10.1016/j.jadohealth.2018.04.007

Arps, E. R., Friesen, M. D., and Overall, N. C. (2018). Promoting youth mental health via text-messages: A New Zealand feasibility study. *Applied Psychology Health and Well-Being*, 10, 457–480. doi:10.1111/aphw.12143

Arseniev-Koehler, A., Lee, H., McCormick, T., and Moreno, M. A. (2016). #Proana: Pro-eating disorder socialization on Twitter. *Journal of Adolescent Health*, 58, 659–664. doi:10.1016/j.jadohealth.2016.02.012

Baker, C. K. and Carreño, P. K. (2016). Understanding the role of technology in adolescent dating and dating violence. *Journal of Child and Family Studies*, 25, 308–320. doi:10.1007/s10826-015-0196-5

Banks, D., Cresswell, J., and Ainley, J. 2003. *Higher-order learning and the use of ICT amongst 15-year olds*. Melbourne, Australia: Australian Council for Educational Research.

Barbero, J. M. (2002). Jóvenes: Comunicación e identidad [Youth: Communication and identity]. *Pensar Iberoamérica: Revista de Cultura*. Retrieved from https://www.oei.es/historico/pensariberoamerica/ric00a03.htm

Bennett, D., Sharpe, M., Freeman, C., and Carson, A. (2004). Anorexia nervosa among female secondary school students in Ghana. *The British Journal of Psychiatry*, 185, 312–317. doi:10.1192/bjp.185.4.312

Bennett, S. J. and Maton, K. A. (2010). Beyond the "digital natives" debate: Towards a more nuanced understanding of students' technology experiences. *Journal of Computer Assisted Learning*, 26, 321–331. doi:10.1111/j.1365-2729.2010.00360.x

Berger, K. S. (2017). *The Developing Person through the Life Span* (10th edition). New York: Worth Publishers.

Berry, J. W. (1980). Acculturation as varieties of adaptation. In A. M. Padilla, ed., *Acculturation: Theories, Models and Findings*. Boulder, CO: Westview, pp. 9–25.

Berry, J. W. (1997). Immigration, acculturation, and adaptation. *Applied Psychology*, 46, 5–34. doi:10.1111/j.1464-0597.1997.tb01087.x

Blais, J. J., Craig, W. M., Pepler, D., and Connolly, J. (2008). Adolescents online: The importance of internet activity choices to salient relationships. *Journal of Youth and Adolescence*, 37, 522–536. doi:10.1007/s10964-007-9262-7

Blakemore, S. J. and Choudhury, S. (2006). Development of the adolescent brain: Implications for executive function and social cognition. *Journal of Child Psychology and Psychiatry*, 47, 296–312. doi:10.1111/j.1469-7610.2006.01611.x

Bond, B. J. (2016). Following your "friend": Social media and the strength of adolescents' parasocial relationships with media personae. *Cyberpsychology, Behavior, and Social Networking*, 19, 656–670. doi:10.1089/cyber.2016.0355

Boniel-Nissim, M., Lenzi, M., Zsiros, E., Gaspar de Matos, M., Gommans, R., Harel-Fisch, Y., et al. (2015). International trends in electronic media communication among 11- to 15-year-olds in 30 countries from 2002 to 2010: Association with ease of communication with friends of the opposite sex. *European Journal of Public Health*, 25, 41–45. doi:10.1093/eurpub/ckv025

Borca, G., Bina, M., Keller, P. S., Gilbert, L. R., and Begotti, T. (2015). Internet use and developmental tasks: Adolescents' point of view. *Computers in Human Behavior*, 52, 49–58. doi:10.1016/j.chb.2015.05.029

Boyd, D. M. and Ellison, N. B. (2007). Social network sites: Definition, history, and scholarship. *Journal of Computer-Mediated Communication*, 13, 210–230. doi:10.1111/j.1083-6101.2007.00393.x

Brenoff, A. (2017). There's no such thing as "digital natives" and the myth that they exist is hurting the entire workforce. *Huffington Post*. Retrieved from https://www.huffpost.com/entry/digital-natives-dontactuallyexist_n_599c985de4b0a296083a9e8a?guccounter=1

Bridge, J. A., Greenhouse, J. B., Ruch, D., Stevens, J., Ackerman, J., Sheftall, A. H., et al. (in press). Association between the release of Netflix's 13 Reasons Why and suicide rates in the United States: An interrupted times series analysis. *Journal of the American Academy of Child & Adolescent Psychiatry*, advance online publication. doi:10.1016/j.jaac.2019.04.020

Brown, B. B. (1999). "You're going out with who?" Peer group influences on adolescent romantic relationships. In W. Furman, B. B. Brown, and

C. Feiring, eds., *The Development of Romantic Relationships in Adolescence*. Cambridge, UK: Cambridge University Press, pp. 291–329.

Brown, J. D. (2000). Adolescents' sexual media diets. *Journal of Adolescent Health*, 27S, 35–40. doi:10.1016/S1054-139X(00)00141–5

Brown, J. D. (2002). Mass media influences on sexuality. *The Journal of Sex Research*, 39, 42–45. doi:10.1080/00224490209552118

Brown, J. D. and Schulze, L. (1990). The effects of race, gender, and fandom on audience interpretations of Madonna's music videos. *Journal of Communication*, 40(2), 88–102. doi:10.1111/j.1460-2466.1990.tb02264.x

Cabré-Riera, A., Torrent, M., Donaire-Gonzalez, D., Vrijheid, M., Cardis, E., and Guxens, M. (2019). Telecommunication devices use, screen time and sleep in adolescents. *Environmental Research*, 171, 341–347. doi:10.1016/j.envres.2018.10.036

Calvani, A., Fini, A., Ranieri, M., and Picci, P. (2012). Are young generations in secondary school digitally competent? A study on Italian teenagers. *Computers & Education*, 58, 797–807. doi:10.1016/j.compedu.2011.10.004

Calvert, S. L., Appelbaum, M., Dodge, K. A., Graham, S., Nagayama Hall, G. C., Hamby, S., et al. (2017). The American Psychological Association Task Force assessment of violent video games: Science in the service of public interest. *American Psychologist*, 72(2), 126–143. doi:10.1037/a0040413

Casaló, L. V. and Escario, J. J. (2019). Predictors of excessive internet use among adolescents in Spain: The relevance of the relationship between parents and their children. *Computers in Human Behavior*, 92, 344–351. doi:10.1016/j.chb.2018.11042

Cejudo, J., López-Delgado, M. L., and Losada, L. (2019). Effectiveness of the videogame "Spock" for the improvement of the emotional intelligence of psychosocial adjustment in adolescents. *Computers in Human Behavior*, 101, 380–386. doi:10.1016/j.chb.2018.09.028

Chang, A. M., Aeschbach, D., Duffy, J. F., and Czeisler, C. A. (2015). Evening use of light-emitting eReaders negatively affects sleep, circadian timing, and next-morning alertness. *Proceedings of the National Academy of Sciences*, 112(4), 1232–1237. doi:10.10.1073/pnas.1418490112

Cheung, C. K. (2016). Media and its influences on adolescents' identity in Hong Kong. In C. K. Cheung, ed., *Media Literacy Education in China*. Singapore: Springer, pp. 105–118.

Cheung, E. (2019). *China Fears That Young People Are Addicted to Video Games. Now It's Imposing a Curfew*. Retrieved from https://edition.cnn.com/2019/11/06/asia/china-bans-online-games-minors-intl-hnk/index.html

Chong, Y. M. G., Teng, K. Z. S., Siew, S. C. A., and Skoric, M. M. (2012). Cultivation effects of video games: A longer-term experimental test of first-

and second-order effects. *Journal of Social and Clinical Psychology*, 31, 952–971. doi:10.1521/jscp.2012.31.9.952

Chu, X. W., Fan, C. Y., Liu, Q. Q., and Zhou, Z. K. (2018). Cyberbullying victimization and symptoms of depression and anxiety among Chinese adolescents: Examining hopelessness as a mediator and self-compassion as a moderator. *Computers in Human Behavior*, 86, 377–386. doi:10.1016/j. chb.2018.04.039

Clow, D. (2013). MOOCs and the funnel of participation. Paper presented at the Conference on Learning Analytics and Knowledge, Leuven, Belgium.

Cohen, J. (2003). Parasocial breakups: Measuring individual differences in responses to the dissolution of parasocial relationships. *Mass Communication & Society*, 6, 191–202. doi:10.1207/S15327825MCS0602_5

Correa, T. (2016). Acquiring a new technology at home: A parent-child study about youths' influence on digital media adoption in a family. *Journal of Broadcasting & Electronic Media*, 60, 123–1390. doi:10.1080/ 08838151.2015.1127238

Coyne, S. M., Padilla-Walker, L. M., and Holmgren, H. G. (2018). A six-year longitudinal study of texting trajectories during adolescence. *Child Development*, 89, 58–65. doi:10.1111/cdv.12823

Craig, S. L. and McInroy, L. (2014). You can form a part of yourself online: The influence of new media on identity development and coming out for LGBTQ youth. *Journal of Gay & Lesbian Mental Health*, 18, 95–109. doi:10.1080/ 19359705.2013.77707

Croucher, S. M. and Kramer, E. (2017). Cultural fusion theory: An alternative to acculturation. *Journal of International and Intercultural Communication*, 10 (2), 97–114. doi:10.1080.17513057.2016.1229498

Crowley, S. J., Wolfson, A. R., Tarokh, L., and Carskadon, M. A. (2018). An update on adolescent sleep: New evidence informing the perfect storm model. *Journal of Adolescence*, 67, 55–65. doi:10.1016/j.adolescence.2018.06.001

Cyberbullying Research Center. (2019). *Cyberbullying: Identification, Prevention, and Response*. Retrieved from https://cyberbullying.org /Cyberbullying-Identification-Prevention-Response-2019.pdf

Davalos, K. M. (1996). "La Quinceañera": Making gender and ethnic identities. *Frontiers: A Journal of Women Studies*, 16, 101–127. doi:10.2307/ 3346805

David-Ferdon, C. and Hertz, M. F. (2007). Electronic media, violence, and adolescents: An emerging public health problem. *Journal of Adolescent Health*, 41, S1–S5. doi:10.1016/j.jadohealth.2007.08.020

DeHart, D., Dwyer, G., Seto, M. C., Moran, R., Letourneau, E., and Schwarz-Watts, D. (2017). Internet sexual solicitation of children:

A proposed typology of offenders based on their chats, e-mails, and social network posts. *Journal of Sexual Aggression*, 23(1), 77–89. doi:10.1080/13552600.2016.1241309

Dias, K. (2003). The ana sanctuary: Women's pro-anorexia narratives in cyberspace. *Journal of International Women's Studies*, 4(2), 31–45. doi:10.1007/s12118-002-1044-0

Dombrowski, S. C., LeMasney, J. W., Ahia, C. E., and Dickson, S. A. (2004). Protecting children from online sexual predators: Technological, psychoeducational, and legal considerations. *Professional Psychology: Research and Practice*, 35(1), 65–73. doi:10.1037/0735-7028.35.1.65

Elias, N. and Lemish, D. (2009). Spinning the web of identity: The roles of the internet in the lives of immigrant adolescents. *New Media & Society*, 11, 1–19. doi:10.1177/1461444809102959

Erikson, S. E., Harrison, K., and Dal Cin, S. (2018). Toward a multi-dimensional model of adolescent romantic parasocial attachment. *Communication Theory*, 28, 376–399. doi:10.1093/ct/qtx006

Exelmans, L. and Van den Bulck, J. (2019). Sleep research: A primer for media scholars. *Health Communication*, 34, 519–528. doi:10.1080/10410236.2017.1422100

Farnham, S. D., Keyes, D., Yuki, V., and Tugwell, C. (2013). Modeling youth civic engagement in a new world of networked publics. In *Proceedings of the Seventh International Association of the Advancements of Artificial Intelligence Conference*. Palo Alto: CA: AAAI Press, pp. 165–174.

Ferguson, C. J. (2007). The good, the bad and the ugly: A meta-analytic review of positive and negative effects of violent video games. *Psychiatric Quarterly*, 78, 309–316. doi:10.1007/s11126-007-9056-9

Ferguson, G. M., Muzaffar, H., Iturbide, M. I., Chu, H., and Meeks Gardner, J. (2018). Feel American, watch American, eat American? Remote acculturation, TV, and nutrition among adolescent–mother dyads in Jamaica. *Child Development*, 89(4), 1360–1377. doi:10.1111/cdev.12808

Ferguson, Y. L., Ferguson, K. T., and Ferguson, G. M. (2017). I am AmeriBritSouthAfrican-Zambian: Multidimensional remote acculturation and well-being among urban Zambian adolescents. *International Journal of Psychology*, 52, 67–76. doi:10.1002/ijop.12191

Flores, X., Gibbons, J. L., and Poelker, K. E. (2016). Generational shifts in the ideals of Guatemalan adolescents. *Psychology and Developing Societies*, 28, 226–250. doi:10.1177/0971333616657172

Flynn, J. R. (1987). Massive IQ gains in 14 nations: What IQ tests really measure. *Psychological Bulletin*, 101, 171–191. doi:10.1037/0033-2909.101.2.171

Friedrich-Cofer, L. and Huston, A. C. (1986). Television violence and aggression: The debate continues. *Psychological Bulletin*, 100, 364–378. doi:10.1037/0033-2909.100.3.364

Frith, S. (1996). Music and identity. In S. Hall and P. Du Gay, eds., *Questions of Cultural Identity*. Thousand Oaks, CA: Sage, pp. 108–127.

Fuchs, T. and Woessmann, L. (2004). Computers and student learning: Bivariate and multivariate evidence on the availability and use of computers at home and at school (CESifo Working Paper, No. 1321). Munich: Center for Economic Studies and Ifo Institute (CESifo).

Fumero, A., Marrero, R. J., Voltes, D., and Peñate, W. (2018). Personal and social factors involved in internet addiction among adolescents: A meta-analysis. *Computers in Human Behavior*, 86, 387–400. doi:10.1016/j.chb.2018.05.005

Gansner, M. E. (2019, September). Gaming addiction in ICD-11: Issues and implications. *Psychiatric Times*. Retrieved from https://www.psychiatrictimes.com/addiction/gaming-addiction-icd-11-issues-and-implications

Gauvain, M. and Munroe, R. L. (2009). Contributions of societal modernity to cognitive development: A comparison of four cultures. *Child Development*, 80(6), 1628–1642. doi:10.1111/j.1467-8624.2009.01358.x

Gentile, D. A. and Gentile, J. R. (2008). Violent video games as exemplary teachers: A conceptual analysis. *Journal of Youth and Adolescence*, 38, 127–141. doi:10.1007/s10964-007-9206-2

Gerbner, G., Gross, L., Morgan, M., and Signorielli, N. (1994). Growing up with television: The cultivation perspective. In J. Bryant and D. Zillmann, eds., *LEA's Communication Series. Media Effects: Advances in Theory and Research*. Hillsdale, NJ: Lawrence Erlbaum Associates, pp. 17–41.

Gibbons, J. L. and Stiles, D. A. (2004). *The Thoughts of Youth: An International Perspective on Adolescents' Ideal Persons*. Greenwich, CT: Information Age.

Ging, D. and Garvey, S. (2018). "Written in these scars are the stories I can't explain": A content analysis of pro-ana and thinspiration image sharing on Instagram. *New Media & Society*, 20(3), 1181–1200. doi:10.1177/1461444816687288

Gleason, T. R., Theran, S. A., and Newberg, E. M. (2017). Parasocial interactions and relationships in early adolescence. *Frontiers in Psychology*, 8, 1–11. doi:10.3389/fpsyg.2017.00255

Greenfield, P. M. (2016). Social change, cultural evolution, and human development. *Current Opinions in Psychology*, 8, 84–92. doi:10.1016/j.copsyc.2015.10.012

Griffiths, M. (2000). Does internet and computer "addiction" exist? Some case study evidence. *Cyberpsychology & Behavior*, 3(2), 211–218. doi:10.1089/109493100316067

Griffiths, M. D., Kuss, D. J., Billieux, J., and Pontes, H. M. (2016). The evolution of internet addiction: A global perspective. *Addictive Behaviors*, 53, 193–195. doi:10.1016/j.addbeh.2015.11.001

Harrington, B. and O'Connell, M. (2016). Video games as virtual teachers: Prosocial video game use by children and adolescents from different socio-economic groups is associated with increased empathy and prosocial behaviour. *Computers in Human Behavior*, 63, 650–658. doi:10.1016/j.chb.2016.05.062

Harrison, K. and Cantor, J. (1997). The relationship between media consumption and eating disorders. *Journal of Communication*, 47, 40–67. doi:10.1111/j.1460-2466.1997.tb02692.x

Heath, M., Sutherland, C., Bartel, K., Gradisar, M., Williamson, P., Lovato, N., et al. (2014). Does one hour of bright or short-wavelength filtered tablet screenlight have a meaningful effect on adolescents' pre-bedtime alertness, sleep, and daytime functioning? *Chronobiology International*, 31, 496–505. doi:10.3109/07420528.2013.872121

Hinduja, S. and Patchin, J. W. (2010). Bullying, cyberbullying, and suicide. *Archives of Suicide Research*, 14, 206–221. doi:10.1080/13811118.2010.494133

Hofstede, G. (2001). *Culture's Consequences: Comparing Values, Behaviors, Institutions and Organizations across Nations* (2nd edition). Thousand Oaks, CA: Sage.

Hollenstein, T. and Lougheed, J. P. (2013). Beyond storm and stress: Typicality, transactions, timing, and temperament to account for adolescent change. *American Psychologist*, 68, 444–454. doi:10.1037/a0033586

Hood, M. M., Vander Wal, J., and Gibbons, J. L. (2009). Culture and eating disorders. In S. Esshun and R. Gurung, eds., *Culture and Mental Health: Sociocultural Influences, Theory, and Practice*. Malden, MA: Blackwell, pp. 273–295.

Huntsinger, C. S., Shaboyan, T., and Karapetyan, A. M. (2019). The influence of globalization on adolescents' conceptions of self and future self in rural and urban Armenia. *New Directions for Child and Adolescent Development*, 164, 1–16. doi:10.1002/cad.20280

Hysing, M., Pallesen, S., Stormark, K. M., Jakobsen, R., Lundervold, A. J., and Sivertsen, B. (2015). Sleep and use of electronic devices in adolescence: Results from a large population-based study. *BMJ Open*, 5, e006748. doi:10.1136/bmjopen-2014-006748

Inglehart, R. and Baker, W. E. (2000). Modernization, cultural change, and the persistence of traditional values. *American Sociological Review*, 65, 19–51. doi:10.2307/2657288

Inglehart, R. F., Ponarin, E., and Inglehart, R. C. (2017). Cultural change, slow and fast: The distinctive trajectory of norms governing gender equality and sexual orientation. *Social Forces*, 95, 1313–1340. doi:10.1093/sf/sox008

Inkeles, A. and Smith, D. (1974). *Becoming Modern: Individual Changes in Six Developing Societies*. Cambridge, MA: Harvard University Press.

International Telecommunications Union. (2019). *Statistics*. Retrieved from https://www.itu.int/en/ITU-D/Statistics/Pages/stat/default.aspx

Irannejad Bisafar, F., Saksono, H., Baquerizo, P., Moore, D., and Parker, A. G. (2016). Youth advocacy in SNAs: Challenges for addressing health disparities. In *Proceedings of the 2016 CHI Conference on Human Factors in Computing Systems*, pp. 3620–3624.

Israelashvili, M., Kim, T., and Bukobza, G. (2012). Adolescents' over-use of the cyber world: Internet addiction or identity exploration? *Journal of Adolescence*, 35, 417–424. doi:10.1016/j.adolescence.2011.07.015

Jacobs, A. (2018, February). In sweeping war on obesity, Chile slays Tony the Tiger. *The New York Times*. Retrieved from https://www.nytimes.com/2018/02/07/health/obesity-chile-sugar-regulations.html

Jacobs, J. (2018, September). Using young adult novels to make sense of #MeToo. *The New York Times*. Retrieved from https://www.nytimes.com/2018/09/12/books/me-too-young-adult-fiction.html

Jakobsson, M., Josefsson, K., Jutengren, G., Sandsjö, L., and Högberg, K. (2019). Sleep duration and sleeping difficulties among adolescents: Exploring associations with school stress, self-perception and technology use. *Scandinavian Journal of Caring Sciences*, 33, 197–206. doi:10.1111/scs.12621

Jensen, L. A. and Arnett, J. J. (2012). Going global: New pathways for adolescents and emerging adults in a changing world. *Journal of Social Issues*, 68, 473–492. doi:10.1111/j.1540-4560.2012.01759.x

Jiang, J. and Kontauts, A. (2019). How social media affect youth civic participation in China. *Regional Formation and Development Studies*, 1, 36–44. doi:10.15181/rfds.v27i1.1866

Jin Jeong, Y., Suh, B., and Gweon, G. (2019). Is smartphone addiction different from internet addiction? Comparison of addiction-risk factors among adolescents. *Behaviour & Information Technology*, advance online publication. doi:10.1080/0144929X.2019.1604805

Jones, K., Williams, J., Sipsma, H., and Patil, C. (2018). Adolescent and emerging adults' evaluation of a Facebook site providing sexual health education. *Populations at Risk Across the Lifespan: Population Studies*, advance online publication. doi:10.1111/phn.12555

Juárez, F. and Gayet, C. (2014). Transitions to adulthood in developing countries. *The Annual Review of Sociology*, 40, 521–538. doi:10.1146/annurev-soc-052914-085540

Jun, S. (2016). The reciprocal longitudinal relationships between mobile phone addiction and depressive symptoms among Korean adolescents. *Computers in Human Behavior*, 58, 179–186. doi:10.1016/j.chb.2015.12.061

Kağıtçıbaşı, C. (2005). Modernization does not mean westernization: Emergence of a different pattern. In W. Friedlmeier, P. Chakkarath, and B. Schwarz, eds., *Culture and Human Development: The Importance of Cross-Cultural Research for the Social Sciences*. Hove: Psychology Press, pp. 255–272.

Kağıtçıbaşı, C. (2017). Doing psychology with a cultural lens: A half-century journey. *Perspectives on Psychological Science*, 12, 824–832. doi:10.1177/1745691617700932

Kamkwamba, W. and Mealer, B. (2009). *The Boy Who Harnessed the Wind*. New York: HarperCollins.

Kapadia, S. (2017). *Adolescence in Urban India: Cultural Construction in a Society in Transition*. New Dehli: Springer.

Katz, E., Blumler, J., and Gurevitch, M. (1974). Utilization of mass communication by the individual. In J. Blumler and E. Katz, eds., *The Uses of Mass Communication: Current Perspectives on Gratifications Research*. Beverly Hills, CA: Sage, pp. 19–34.

Kimball, G. (2019). *Global Youth Transforming Our Future*. Vancouver: Equality Press.

King, D. L., Gradisar, M., Drummond, A., Lovato, N., Wessel, J., Micic, G., et al. (2013). The impact of prolonged violent video-gaming on adolescent sleep: An experimental study. *Journal of Sleep Research*, 22, 137–143. doi:10.1111/j.1365-2869.2012.01060.x

Kirschner, P. A. and De Bruyckere, P. (2017). The myths of the digital native and the multitasker. *Teaching and Teacher Evaluation*, 67, 135–142. doi:10.1016/j.tate.2017.06.001

Kojima, R., Sato, M., Akiyama, Y., Shinohara, R., Mizorogi, S., Suzuki, K., et al. (2019). Problematic internet use and its associations with health-related symptoms and lifestyle habits among rural Japanese adolescents. *Psychiatry and Clinical Neurosciences*, 73, 20–26. doi:10.1111/pcn.12791

Koutamanis, M., Vossen, H. G. M., Peter, J., and Valkenburg, P. M. (2013). Practice makes perfect: The longitudinal effect of adolescents' instant messaging on their ability to initiate offline friendships. *Computers in Human Behavior*, 29, 2265–2272. doi:10.1016/j.chb.2013.04.033

Kraut, R., Lundmark, V., Patterson, M., Kiesler, S., Mukopadhyay, T., and Scherlis, W. (1998). Internet paradox: A social technology that reduces social involvement and psychological well-being? *American Psychologist*, 53, 1017e1031. doi:10.1037//0003-066X.53.9.1017

Krayer, A., Ingledew, D. K., and Iphofen, R. (2007). Social comparison and body image in adolescence: A grounded theory approach. *Health Education Research*, 23, 892–903. doi:10.1093/her/cym076

Kross, E., Verduyn, P., Demiralp, E., Park, J., Lee, D. S., Lin, N., et al. (2013). Facebook use predicts declines in subjective wellbeing in young adults. *PLOS One*, 8, e69841. doi:10.1371/journal.pone.0069841

Larson, R. (1995). Secrets in the bedroom: Adolescents' private use of media. *Journal of Youth and Adolescence*, 24, 535–550. doi:10.1007/BF01537055

Lau, P. W. C., Lau, E. Y., Wong, D. P., and Ransdell, L. (2011). A systematic review of information and communication technology-based interventions for promoting physical activity behavior change in children and adolescents. *Journal of Medical Internet Research*, 13, e48. doi:10.2196/jmir.1533

LeBourgeois, M. K., Hale, L., Chang, A. M., Akacem, L. D., Montgomery-Downs, H. E., and Buxton, O. M. (2017). Digital media and sleep in childhood and adolescence. *Pediatrics*, 140(Supplement 2), S92. doi:10.1542/peds.2016-1758J

Leming, J. S. (1987). Rock music and the socialization of moral values in early adolescence. *Youth and Society*, 18, 363–383. doi:10.1177/0044118X87018004004

Lerner, R. M. (2008). *The Good Teen: Rescuing Adolescence from the Myths of the Storm and Stress Years*. New York: Three Rivers Press.

Leung, L. (2011). Loneliness, social support, and preference for online social interaction: The mediating effects of identity experimentation online among children and adolescents. *Chinese Journal of Communication*, 4, 381–399. doi:10.1080/17544750.2012.616285

Levine, M. P. and Smolak, L. (2016). The role of protective factors in the prevention of negative body image and disordered eating. *Eating Disorders*, 24, 39–46. doi:10.1080/10640266.2015.1113826

Liang, L., Zhou, D., Yuan, C., Shao, A., and Bian, Y. (2016). Gender differences in the relationship between internet addiction and depression: A cross-lagged study in Chinese adolescents. *Computers in Human Behavior*, 63, 463–470. doi:10.1016/j.chb.2016.04.043

Lorenzo-Blanco, E. I., Arillo-Santillán, E., Unger, J. B., and Thrasher, J. (2019). Remote acculturation and cigarette smoking susceptibility among youth in

Mexico. *Journal of Cross-Cultural Psychology*, 50, 63–79. doi:10.1177/0022022118807578

Lu, W. (2018, April). What #MeToo means to teenagers. *The New York Times*. Retrieved from https://www.nytimes.com/2018/04/19/well/family/metoo-me-too-teenagers-teens-adolescents-high-school.html

Manago, A. (2014). Connecting societal change to value differences across generations: Adolescents, mothers, and grandmothers in a Maya community in southern Mexico. *Journal of Cross-Cultural Psychology*, 45, 868–887. doi:10.1177/0022022114527346

Manago, A. M. and Pacheco, P. (2019). Globalization and the transition to adulthood in a Maya community in Mexico: Communication technologies, social networks, and views on gender. In J. McKenzie, ed., *Globalization as a Context for Youth Development: New Directions for Child and Adolescent Development*. doi:10.1002/cad.20273

Marino, C. (2018). Quality of social-media use may matter more than frequency of use for adolescents' depression. *Clinical Psychological Science*, 6, 455. doi:10.1177/2167702618771979

Martins, M. J. D., Veiga Simão, A. M., Freire, I., Cactano, A. P., and Matos, A. (2016). Cyber-victimization and cyber-aggression among Portuguese adolescents: The relation to family support and family rules. *International Journal of Cyber Behavior, Psychology and Learning*, 6, 65–78. doi:10.4018/IJCBPI.2016070105

Marwick, A. E. (2008). To catch a predator? The MySpace moral panic. *First Monday*, 13(6). Retrieved from https://journals.uic.edu/ojs/index.php/fm/article/view/2152

Mazalin, D. and Moore, S. (2004). Internet use, identity development and social anxiety among young adults. *Behaviour Change*, 21, 90–102. doi:10.1375/bech.21.2.90.55425

McCabe, M. P., Ricciardelli, L. A., and Ridge, D. (2006). "Who thinks I need a perfect body?" Perceptions and internal dialogue among adolescents about their bodies. *Sex Roles*, 55, 409–419. doi:10.1007/s11199-006-9093-0

McLaughlin, C. (2016). *The Homework Gap: The "Cruelest Part of the Digital Divide."* Retrieved from http://neatoday.org/2016/04/20/the-homework-gap

McLean, S. A., Paxton, S. J., and Wertheim, E. H. (2016). Does media literacy mitigate risk for reduced body satisfaction following exposure to thin-ideal media? *Journal of Youth and Adolescence*, 45, 1678–1695. doi:10.1007/s10964-016-0440-3

McQuail, D. (1994). The rise of media of mass communication. In D. McQuail, ed., *Mass Communication Theory: An Introduction*. London: Sage, pp. 1–29.

Mead, M. (1928). *Coming of Age in Samoa*. New York: Morrow.

Mensch, B., Bruce, J., and Greene, E. M. (1998) *The Uncharted Passage: Girls' Adolescence in the Developing World*. New York: Population Council.

Mireku, M. O., Barker, M. M., Mutz, J., Dumontheil, I., Thomas, M. S., Röösli, M., et al. (2019). Night-time screen-based media device use and adolescents' sleep and health-related quality of life. *Environment International*, 124, 66–78. doi:10.1016/j.envint.2018.11.069

Mitchell, K., Jones, L., Finkelhor, D., and Wolak, J. (2014). *Trends in Unwanted Sexual Solicitations: Findings from the Youth Internet Safety Studies*. Durham, NH: Crimes Against Children Research Center. Retrieved from http://www.unh.edu/ccrc/pdf/Sexual%20Solicitation%201%20of%204%20YISS%20Bulletins%20Feb%202014.pdf

Monge Benito, S. and Olabarri Fernández, M. E. (2011). Los alumnos de la UPV/EHU frente a Tuenti y Facebook: Usos y percepciones [The students of UPV/EHU regarding Tuenti y Facebook: Uses and perceptions]. *Revista Latina de Comunicación Social*, 66, 79–100. doi:10.4185/RLCS-66-2011-925079-100

Moreno, M. A. and Whitehill, J. M. (2014). Influence of social media on alcohol use in adolescents and young adults. *Alcohol Research: Current Reviews*, 36, 91–100.

Moreno-Ruiz, D., Martínez-Ferrer, B., and García-Bacete, F. (2019). Parenting styles, cyberaggression, and cybervictimization among adolescents. *Computers in Human Behavior*, 93, 252–259. doi:10.1016/j.chb.2018.12.031

Mukhongo, L. L. (2014). Negotiating the new media platforms: Youth and political images in Kenya. *tripleC*, 12, 328–341. doi:10.31269/triplec.v12i1.509

National Centre for Educational Statistics. (2001a). *The Nation's Report Card: Mathematics 2000*. Washington, DC: NCES.

National Centre for Educational Statistics. (2001b). *The Nation's Report Card: Science 2000*. Washington, DC: NCES.

Nichter, M. (2009). *Fat Talk*. Cambridge, MA: Harvard University Press.

Nickerson, R. S. (1998). Confirmation bias: A ubiquitous phenomenon in many guises. *Review of General Psychology*, 2, 175–220. doi:10.1037/1089-2680.2.2.175

Offer, D. Ostrov, E., Howard, K. I., and Atkinson, R. (1988). *The Teenage World: Adolescents' Self-Image in Ten Countries*. New York: Plenum Medical.

Olson, L., Daggs, J., Ellevold, B., and Rogers, T. (2007). Entrapping the innocent: Toward a theory of child sexual predators' luring communication. *Communication Theory*, 17, 231–251. doi:10.1111/j.1468-2885.2007.00294.x

Ophir, Y., Asterhan, C. S. C., and Schwarz, B. B. (2019). The digital footprints of adolescent depression, social rejection and victimization of bullying on Facebook. *Computers in Human Behavior*, 91, 62–71. doi:10.1016/j.chb.2018.09.025

Orben, A. and Przybylski, A. K. (2019). Screens, teens, and psychological well-being: Evidence from three time-use-diary studies. *Psychological Science*, 30, 682–696. doi:10.1177/0956797619830329

Organisation for Economic Co-operation and Development. (2015). *Students, Computers and Learning: Making the Connection*. Paris: OECD.

Owston, R. D. (1997). The world wide web: A technology to enhance teaching and learning. *Research News and Comment*, 26, 27–33. doi:10.3102.0013189X026002027

Pacheco, E. and Melhuish, N. (2018). *New Zealand Teens' Digital Profile: A Factsheet*. Retrieved from https://www.netsafe.org.nz/youth-factsheet-2018

Pargament, K. I., Poloma, M. M., and Tarakeshwar, N. (2001). Methods of coping from the religions of the world: The Bar Mitzvah, karma, and spiritual health. In C. R. Synder, ed., *Coping with Stress: Effective People and Processes*. New York: Oxford University Press, pp. 259–284.

Pegrum, M., Oakley, G., and Faulkner, R. (2013). Schools going mobile: A study of the adoption of mobile handheld technologies in Western Australian independent schools. *Australasian Journal of Educational Technology*, 29, 66–81. doi:10.14742/ajet.64

Pence, A. (2015). Mobilizing literacy: Cell phones help Afghan women learn to read. *Solutions*, 6, 8–9.

Pennebaker, J. W. (1997). Writing about emotional experiences as a therapeutic process. *Psychological Science*, 8, 162–166. doi:10.1111/j.1467-9280.1997.tb00403.x

Pérez Sánchez, R. (2019). *Niñas, niños y adolescentes en la internet*. Retrieved from http://globalkidsonline.net/wp-content/uploads/2019/07/Kids-Online-Costa-Rica-1-Julio.pdf

Petersen, A. C., Silbereisen, R. K., and Sorensen, S. (1996). Adolescent development: A global perspective. In K. Hurrelmann and S. F. Hamilton, eds., *Social Problems and Social Contexts in Adolescence: Perspectives across Boundaries*. New York: Aldine de Gruyter, pp. 3–37.

Poelker, K. E., Gibbons, J. L., Maxwell, C., and Elizondo Quintanilla, I. L. (2017). Envy, gratitude, and well-being among Guatemalan adolescents with scarce economic resources. *International Perspectives in Psychology: Research, Practice, Consultation*, 6, 209–226. doi:10.1037/ipp0000076

Prensky, M. (2001). Digital natives, digital immigrants (Part 1). *On the Horizon*, 9, 1–6. doi:10.1108/10748120110424816

Ranosa, T. (2016, March). Teens now using Google Docs as chat app. *Tech Times*. Retrieved from https://www.techtimes.com/articles/239731/20190316/teens-now-using-google-docs-as-chat-app.htm

Rao, M. A., Berry, R., Gonsalves, A., Hostak, Y., Shah, M., and Roeser, R. W. (2013). Globalization and the identity remix among adolescents. *Journal of Research on Adolescence*, 23, 9–24. doi:10.1111/jora.12002

Rehbein, F., Kliem, S., Baier, D., Mößle, T., and Petry, N. M. (2015). Prevalence of internet gaming disorder in German adolescents: Diagnostic contribution of the nine DSM-5 criteria in a state-wide representative sample. *Addiction*, 110, 842–851. doi:10.1111/add.12849.

Riddle, K. (2010). Always on my mind: Exploring how frequent, recent, and vivid television portrayals are used in the formation of social reality judgments. *Media Psychology*, 13, 155–179. doi:10.1080/15213261003800140

Roberts, D. F. and Bachen, C. M. (1981). Mass communication effects. *Annual Review of Psychology*, 32, 307–356. doi:10.1146/annurev.ps.32.020181.001515

Rogers, K. (2016, July). The "ice bucket challenge" helped scientists discover a new gene tied to ALS. *The New York Times*. Retrieved from https://www.nytimes.com/2016/07/28/health/the-ice-bucket-challenge-helped-scientists-discover-a-new-gene-tied-to-als.html

Rokicki, S., Cohen, J., Salomon, J. A., and Fink, G. (2017). Impact of a text message program on adolescent reproductive health: A cluster-randomized trial in Ghana (UCD Geary Institute for Public Policy discussion paper series). Dublin: University College Dublin, Geary Institute.

Romera, E. M., Herrera-López, M., Casas, J. A., Ortega-Ruiz, R., and Gómez-Ortiz, O. (2017). Multidimensional social competence, motivation, and cyberbullying: A cultural approach with Colombian and Spanish adolescents. *Journal of Cross-Cultural Psychology*, 48, 1183–1197. doi:10.1177/0022022116687854

Rössler, P. and Brosius, H. B. (2001). Do talk shows cultivate adolescents' views of the world? A prolonged-exposure experiment. *Journal of Communication*, 51, 143–163. doi:10.1111/j.1460-2466-2001.tb02876.x

Rossmann, C. and Brosius, H. B. (2004). The problem of causality in cultivation research. *Communications-European Journal of Communication Research*, 29, 379–397. doi:10.1515/comm.2004.024

Ruggiero, T. E. (2000). Uses and gratifications theory in the 21st century. *Mass Communication & Society*, 3, 3–37. doi:10.1207/S15327825MCS0301_02

Ruggiero, K. J., Price, M., Adams, Z., Stauffacher, K., McCauley, J., Danielson, C. K., et al. (2015). Web intervention for adolescents affected by disaster: Population-based randomized controlled trial. *Journal of the American Academy of Child & Adolescent Psychiatry*, 54, 709–717. doi:10.1016/j.jaac.2015.07.001.

Saloman, A. and Kolikant, Y. B.-D. (2016). High-school students' perceptions of the effects of non-academic usage of ICT on their academic achievements. *Computers in Human Behavior*, 64, 143–151. doi:10.1016/j.chb.2016.06.024

San Clemente, N. and Cote, T. (2018). *Adolescent Online Safety and Behavior Report*. Retrieved from https://static1.squarespace.com/static/5809286abe6594e82df59790/t/5b608417352f53c1e4e371bf/1533051933502/Adolescent+online+safety+and+behavior+report+EDIT+FINAL.pdf

Satterwhite, C. L., Torrone, E., Meites, E., Dunne, E. F., Mahajan, R., Bañez Ocfemia, M. C., et al. (2013). Sexually transmitted infections among US women and men: Prevalence and incidence estimates, 2008. *Sexually Transmitted Diseases*, 40, 187–193. doi:10.1097/OLQ.0b013e318286bb53

Schlegel, A. (2000). The global spread of adolescent culture. In L. J. Crockett and R. K. Silbereisen, eds., *Negotiating Adolescence in Times of Social Change*. Cambridge, UK: Cambridge University Press, pp. 71–88.

Schlegel, A. and Barry, H. (1991). *Adolescence: An Anthropological Inquiry*. New York: Free Press.

Seate. A. A. and Mastro, D. (2016). Media's influence on immigration attitudes: An intergroup threat theory approach. *Communication Monographs*, 83, 194–213. doi:10.1080/03637751.2015.1068433.

Shamim, I. (2017). Child sexual abuse and exploitation online in Bangladesh: The challenges of the internet and law and legal developments. In S. Shahidullah, ed., *Crime, Criminal Justice, and the Evolving Science of Criminology in South Asia*. London: Palgrave Macmillan, pp. 145–171.

Shukor, S. A., Abd, H., Shah, R., and Musa, N. A. (2017). Regulating children's safety on the internet: A Malaysian perspective. *International Journal for Studies on Children, Women, Elderly and Disabled People*, 1, 152–156.

Siibak, A. and Tamme, V. (2013). "Who introduced Granny to Facebook?": An exploration of everyday family interactions in web-based communication environments. *Northern Lights*, 11, 71–89. doi:10.1386/nl.11.1.71_

Steele, J. R. and Brown, J. D. (1995). Adolescent room culture: Studying media in the context of everyday life. *Journal of Youth and Adolescence*, 24, 551–576. doi:10.1007/BF01537056

Stice, E. and Bearman, S. K. (2001). Body-image and eating disturbances prospectively predict increases in depressive symptoms in adolescent girls:

A growth curve analysis. *Developmental Psychology*, 37, 597–607. doi:10.1037/0012-1649.37.5.597

Stice, E., Schupak-Neuberg, E., Shaw, H. E., and Stein, R. I. (1994). Relation of media exposure to eating disorder symptomatology: An examination of mediating mechanisms. *Journal of Abnormal Psychology*, 103, 836–840. doi:10.1037/0021-843X.103.4.836

Stonard, K. E., Bowen, E., Walker, K., and Price, S. A. (2017). "They always find a way to get to you": Technology use in adolescent romantic relationships in its role in dating violence and abuse. *Journal of Interpersonal Violence*, 32, 2083–2117. doi:10.1177/0886260515590787

Subrahmanyam, K. and Greenfield, P. (2008). Online communication and adolescent relationships. *The Future of Children*, 18, 119–146. doi:10.1352/foc.0.0006

Suler, J. (2004). The online disinhibition effect. *Cyberpsychology & Behavior*, 7, 321–326. doi:10.1089/1094931041291295

Symons, K., Ponnet, K., Walrave, M., and Heirman, W. (2017). A qualitative study into parental mediation of adolescents' internet use. *Computers in Human Behavior*, 73, 423–432. doi:10.1016/j.chb.2017.04.004

Tamme, V. and Siibak, A. (2012). Enhancing family cohesion through web-based communication: Analysis of online communication practices in Estonian families. *Observatorio*, 1–28. doi:10.15847/obsOBS000581

Tandoc, E. C., Ferruci, P., and Duffy, M. (2015). Facebook use, envy, and depression among college students: Is facebooking depression? *Computers in Human Behavior*, 43, 139–146. doi:10.1016/j.chb.2014.10.053

Te'Eni-Hararia, T. and Eyalb, K. (2019). The role of food advertising in adolescents' nutritional health socialization. *Health Communication*, advance online publication. doi:10.1080/10410236.2019.1598737

Thackeray, R. and Hunter, M. A. (2010). Empowering youth: Use of technology in advocacy to affect social change. *Journal of Computer-Mediated Communication*, 15, 575–591. doi:10.1111/j.1083-6101.2009.01503.x

Thinyane, H., (2010). Are digital natives a world-wide phenomenon? An investigation into South African first year students' use and experience with technology. *Computers & Education*, 55, 406–414. doi:10.1016/j.compedu.2010.02.005

Tukachinsky, R. and Dorros, S. M. (2018). Parasocial romantic relationships, romantic beliefs, and relationship outcomes in USA adolescents: Rehearsing love or setting oneself up to fail? *Journal of Children and Media*, 12, 329–345. doi:10.1080/17482798.2018.1463917

Tulane, S., Vaterlaus, J. M., and Beckert, T. E. (2017). An A in their social lives, but an F in school: Adolescent perceptions of texting in school. *Youth & Society*, 49, 711–732. doi:10.1177/0044118X14559916

Twenge, J. M. (2017). *iGen: Why Today's Super-Connected Kids Are Growing up Less Rebellious, More Tolerant, Less Happy – and Completely Unprepared for Adulthood – and What That Means for the Rest of Us.* New York: Atria Books.

Twenge, J. M., Hisler, G. C., and Krizan, Z. (2019). Associations between screen time and sleep duration are primarily driven by portable electronic devices: Evidence from a population-based study of US children ages 0–17. *Sleep Medicine*, 56, 211–218. doi:10.1016/j.sleep.2018.11.009

Twenge, J. M., Joiner, T. E., Rogers, M. L., and Martin, G. N. (2018). Increases in depressive symptoms, suicide-related outcomes, and suicide rates among US adolescents after 2010 and links to increased new media screen time. *Clinical Psychological Science*, 6, 3–17. doi:10.1177/2167702617723376

Twenge, J. M., Martin, G. N., and Spitzberg, B. H., (2019). Trends in US adolescents' media use, 1976–2016: The rise of digital media, the decline of TV, and the (near) demise of print. *Psychology of Popular Media Culture*, 8(4), 329. doi:10.1037/ppm0000203

Uhls, Y. T., Ellison, N. B., and Subrahmanyam, K. (2017). Benefits and costs of social media in adolescence. *Pediatrics*, 140(Supplement 2), S67–S70. doi:10.1542/peds.2016-1758E

UNESCO. (2011). *Transforming Education: The Power of ICT Policies.* Paris: United Nations Educational, Scientific and Cultural Organization.

UNICEF. (2017). *The State of the World's Children 2017: Children in a Digital World.* New York: United Nations.

UNICEF. (2018). *Adolescents Overview.* Retrieved from https://data.unicef.org/topic/adolescents/overview/

Valkenburg, P. M. and Peter, J. (2008). Adolescents' identity experiments on the internet: Consequences for social competence and self-concept unity. *Communication Research*, 35, 208–231. doi:10.1177/0093650207313164

Valkenburg, P. M. and Peter, J. (2006). Friend networking sites and their relationship to adolescents' well-being and social self-esteem. *CyberBullying & Behavior*, 9, 584–590. doi:10.1089/cpb.2006.9.584

Valkenburg, P. M., Schouten, A. P., and Peter, J. (2005). Adolescents' identity exploration on the internet. *New Media Society*, 7, 383–402. doi:10.1177/1461444805052282

Valkenburg, P. M., Peter, J., and Schouten, A. P. (2006). Friend networking sites and their relationship to adolescents' well-being and social self-esteem. *CyberPsychology & Behavior*, 9, 584–590. doi:10.1089/cpb.2006.9.584

Vandendriessche, A., Ghekiere, A., Van Cauwenberg, J., De Clercq, B., Dhondt, K., DeSmet, A., et al. (2019). Does sleep mediate the association between school pressure, physical activity, screen time, and psychological symptoms in early adolescents? A 12-country study. *International Journal of Environmental Research and Public Health*, 16(6), 1–15. doi:10.3390/ijerph16061072

Van der Lely, S., Frey, S., Garbazza, C., Wirz-Justice, A., Jenni, O. G., Steiner, R., et al. (2015). Blue blocker glasses as a countermeasure for alerting effects of evening light-emitting diode screen exposure in male teenagers. *Journal of Adolescent Health*, 56, 113–119. doi:10.1016/j.jadohealth.2014.08.002

Vander Wal, J., Gibbons, J. L., and Grazioso, M. P. (2008). The sociocultural model of eating disorder development: Application to a Guatemalan sample. *Eating Behaviors*, 9, 277–284. doi:10.1016/j.eatbeh.2007.10.002

Van Ouytsel, J., Van Gool, E., Walrave, M., Ponnet, K., and Peeters, E. (2015). Exploring the role of social networking sites within adolescent romantic relationships and dating experiences. *Computers in Human Behavior*, 55, 76–86. doi:10.1016/j.chb.2015.08.042

Vermeulen, A., Vanderbosch, H., and Heirman, W. (2018). #Smiling, #venting, or both? Adolescents' social sharing of emotions on social media. *Computers in Human Behavior*, 84, 211–219. doi:10.1016/j.chb.2018.02.022

Vossen, H. G. M. and Valkenburg, P. M. (2016). Do social media foster or curtail adolescents' empathy? A longitudinal study. *Computers in Human Behavior*, 63, 118–124. doi:10.1016/j.chb.2016.05.040

Wang, X., Yang, J., Wang, P., and Lei, L. (2019). Childhood maltreatment, moral disengagement, and adolescents' cyberbullying perpetuation: Fathers' and mothers' moral disengagement as moderators. *Computers in Human Behavior*, 95, 48–57. doi:10.1016/j.chb.2019.01.031

Warren, A. M., Jaafar, N. I., and Sulaiman, A. (2016). Youth civic engagement behavior on Facebook: A comparison of findings from Malaysia and Indonesia. *Journal of Global Information Technology Management*, 19, 128–142. doi:10.1080/1097198X.2016.1187527

Weaver, E., Gradisar, M., Dohnt, H., Lovato, N., and Douglas, P. (2010). The effect of presleep video-game playing on adolescent sleep. *Journal of Clinical Sleep Medicine*, 6, 184–189.

Weinstock, M., Ganayiem, M., Igbariya, R., Manago, A. M., and Greenfield, P. M. (2015). Societal change and values in Arab communities in Israel: Intergenerational and rural- urban comparisons. *Journal of Cross-Cultural Psychology*, 46, 19–38. doi:10.1177/0022022114551792

White, R. D. (2017). *Youth and Society*. South Melbourne: Oxford University Press.

Wichstrøm, L., Stenseng, F., Belsky, J., von Soest, T., and Hygen, B. W. (2019). Symptoms of Internet Gaming Disorder in youth: Predictors and comorbidity. *Journal of Abnormal Child Psychology*, 47, 71–83. doi:10.1007/s10802-018-0422-x

Widman, L., Nesi, J., Kamke, K., Choukas-Bradley, S., and Stewart, J. L. (2018). Technology-based interventions to reduce sexually transmitted infections and unintended pregnancies among youth. *Journal of Adolescent Health*, 62, 651–660. doi:10.1016/j.jadohealth.2018.02.007

Wolak, J., Finkelhor, D., Mitchell, K. J., and Ybarra, M. L. (2008). Online "predators" and their victims: Myths, realities, and implications for prevention and treatment. *American Psychologist*, 63, 111–128. doi:10.1037/0003-066X.63.2.111

Woodcock, B., Middleton, A., and Nortcliffe, A. (2012). Considering the smartphone learning: Developing innovation to investigate the opportunities for students and their interest. *Student Engagement and Experience Journal*, 1, 1–15. doi:10.7190/seej.v1i1.38

World Health Organization. (2014). *Global Youth Tobacco Survey*. Retrieved from http://www.tobaccoatlas.org/topic/smoking-among-youth/

World Possible. (n.d.) *Our Story*. Retrieved from https://worldpossible.org/story

Wright, M. F. (2015). Cyber victimization and adjustment difficulties: The mediation of Chinese and American adolescents' digital technology usage. *Cyberpsychology: Journal of Psychosocial Research on Cyberspace*, 9(1). doi:10.5817/CP2015-1-7

Ybarra, M. L., Diener-West, M., and Leaf, P. J. (2010). Examining the overlap in internet harassment and school bullying: Implications for school intervention. *Journal of Adolescent Health*, 41, S42–S50. doi:10.1016/j.jadohealth.2007.09.004

Young, R., Len-Ríos, M., and Young, H. (2017). Romantic motivations for social media use, social comparison, and online aggression among adolescents. *Computers in Human Behavior*, 75, 385–395. doi:10.1016/j.chb.2017.04.021

Cambridge Elements ⹀

Psychology and Culture

Kenneth D. Keith

University of San Diego

Kenneth D. Keith is author or editor of more than 160 publications on cross-cultural psychology, quality of life, intellectual disability, and the teaching of psychology. He was the 2017 president of the Society for the Teaching of Psychology.

About the Series

Elements in Psychology and Culture features authoritative surveys and updates on key topics in cultural, cross-cultural, and indigenous psychology. Authors are internationally recognized scholars whose work is at the forefront of their subdisciplines within the realm of psychology and culture.

Cambridge Elements ⁼

Psychology and Culture

Elements in the Series

A full series listing is available at: www.cambridge.org/EPAC

4181

CPSIA information can be obtained
at www.ICGtesting.com
Printed in the USA
LVHW010743190420
653724LV00010B/162